10 Minutes for Talking

How to Raise a Strong Communicator in 10 Minutes a Day

Amy Maschue, M.S. CCC-SLP
Speech-Language Pathologist
Mom of 6

ABOUT THE AUTHOR

Amy Maschue is a certified speech-language pathologist practicing in Phoenix, Arizona. She specializes in helping children with Autism Spectrum Disorder and other early language-learning difficulties become effective communicators by engaging them in real dialogues that provide a language rich environment to notice and practice new conversational language skills. As a mom of six, Amy realized that the same dialogue building principles she used with her clients promoted advanced communication development in her young children. *10 Minutes for Talking: How to Raise a Strong Communicator in 10 Minutes a Day* gives you 200+ of Amy's practical, professional, mom-tested ideas for MAXIMIZING YOUR CHILD'S COMMUNICATION POTENTIAL in the formative first four years.

DEDICATION
To my husband, Phil, and six children Tommy, Anne Marie, Philip, Jillian, Maeve and Jason. Communicating with you makes my day.
I love you!

Copyright © 2012 Amy Maschue
All rights reserved.
ISBN-10: 0615681050
ISBN-13: 9780615681054

CONTENTS

INTRODUCTION		4
INFANT TALK		9
	How Infants Communicate: Birth to 1 yr	10
	Daily Activities that Maximize Communication	15
	Using Signs to Facilitate Communication	26
BABY TALK		28
	How Babies Communicate: 1 yr to 2 yrs	29
	Daily Activities that Maximize Communication	35
	How to Maximize Communication by Facilitating Sound System Development	46
TODDLER TALK		49
	How Toddlers Communicate: 2 yrs to 3 yrs	50
	Daily Activities that Maximize Communication	57
	How to Maximize Communication by Facilitating Grammatical Development	68
PRESCHOOLER TALK		70
	How Preschoolers Communicate: 3yrs to 5 yrs	71
	Daily Activities that Maximize Communication	78
	How to Maximize Communication by Facilitating the Development of Dramatic Play	89
F.Y.I	How Books Maximize Communication Now and in the Future	91
	Notes and References	94

INTRODUCTION

Welcome parents and caregivers! My name is Amy Maschue, M.S. CCC-SLP. As a mom of six children and certified speech-language pathologist (SLP), I am excited to share with you practical, proven ways to maximize your child's communication skills in everyday activities.

Over the course of my career as an SLP specializing in early childhood language development, I have designed curriculum and provided intervention for individual and group-based programs. My work in research, public education, clinic and private home settings brought me to a realization that formed my intervention philosophy. Because I had limited time with each child, teaching the parents and siblings the strategies that best facilitated communication development was the most efficient way to make communication gains. This strategy, often called an indirect-therapy model (Hegde, 1996), had another predictable outcome that turned out to be especially important for the children I had on my caseload.

Almost 90% of the kids on my caseload had been diagnosed with Autism Spectrum Disorder and struggled with communication acquisition in general, but specifically with conversational language skills. The more people I taught to use specific language-promoting strategies with the child, the more versed the child became in specific speech and language skills. As the child increased his competency in conversation, he became more confident, and therefore comfortable, in having and even seeking out conversations.

Most children have typically-developing communication skills. In the course of their daily lives they are naturally tuned into the speech and language patterns used by any and all who communicate with them. As a SLP, I watch a child learning to use/express his ideas and marvel in the miracle! In four short years a child goes from only being able to cry and gaze to communicating in full dialogues. Along the way the child learns and tests the communication patterns he hears, like:

- First, finding that *you do something to get something* (e.g., in his first year by looking at mommy and reaching

towards a ball on a shelf in order to request the ball).
- Second, noticing that **words work** (e.g., by saying "banana" to get a banana sometime around his first birthday).
- Third, **putting words together to express his understanding that his opinion differs from yours**, aka early perspective taking (e.g., around age 2 when he protests sharing a toy by saying, "No mine!").
- Fourth, **using words to socialize and entertain** (e.g., in his third year by pretending to be Mommy or Dad on the phone or trying tirelessly to tell about what he saw at the park).
- Fifth, understanding that not only do others think about things differently than he does, but realizing that **he can learn why by asking and even influence another's ideas by sharing his own** (e.g., in his fourth year when he asks why you like purple popsicles when he likes red and suggests that you might like red if you just tasted it).

Because this communication journey is so natural, you may ask yourself, "What are the benefits of maximizing the typical-language development of my child?" It's a good question. My answer is best illustrated in a simple question of my own: Think about a time where you had difficulty being understood, getting your message across to another person…How did it feel? Likely your answer is, "It felt frustrating". It feels frustrating for a child too! Look at your child and you will likely notice that he seems to "know" more than he can talk about. While this pattern of having a higher "understanding" or "knowledge" of language (called receptive language) than what can be expressed (called expressive language) is typical, it often naturally leads to some communicative frustration (Hegde, 1996). This frustration in a child manifests in tantrums, crying and sometimes other physical behaviors like biting or hitting. The main benefit of maximizing your child's natural communication potential is two-fold:

1. You are <u>increasing</u> your child's ability to communicate ideas about the world with others. Success in doing so gives your child a sense of self-esteem and a plethora of positive communication experiences that will encourage more communication and expression.

2. You are <u>decreasing</u> your child's communicative frustration by providing an arsenal of tools from which a communication breakdown can be avoided (i.e., he has the words to ask and get his needs met) or noticed and quickly dealt with (i.e., when he points to the toys on the shelf to request the ball and instead gets a train, he puts the train aside and says, "ball"), leaving the interaction having ultimate success getting his needs and wants met.

When I had my first child, I was excited to use the communication-promoting strategies I had honed in my professional life to maximize my child's communication potential. I began implementing speech and language promoting strategies into all of our daily activities: diaper changing, meal times, bath time, book reading, playing with toys, etc. It worked. My oldest son was an early communicator: nonverbal turntaking (e.g., moving arms and cooing to initiate tickles) in interactions as early as two months, using signs to communicate his needs/wants around age nine months and using spoken words consistently by 10 months. Many of my friends with kids noticed my son's advanced communication and were delighted at the easy-to-implement suggestions I had for them to do the same with their children. Now on number six, I can say that it gets easier to implement these strategies the more "helpers" you have. My older children act as peer models for the younger ones and all are excited to help the youngest.

In *10 Minutes for Talking*, I have listed common, everyday activities in the lives of young children. Under each activity there are suggestions for parents and caregivers that will allow them to maximize the communication potential of these situations. Each of these 200+ suggestions take less than 10 minutes to implement, but encourage interactions that are language-rich and fun, so you may find yourself engaging your child for longer!

I suggest choosing one or two activities each day in which you consciously focus on promoting communication skills. In so doing, you will be more apt to notice the level of your child's communication skills and help him maximize his communication potential!

Key to using these activities in the most enriching way for your child is noticing where his speech and language skills are currently and identifying which skill he should acquire next. If we want to maximize the development of communication skills we need to take advantage of established skills while introducing new ones. This philosophy is called keeping interactions at your child's "growing edge." When you use communication-promoting strategies to focus your child's attention on "growing edge" skills, you support your child noticing and practicing the next developmentally-appropriate skill.

So, how do you know where your child's "growing edge" of communication development is? I start the search for a child's "growing edge" by identifying which stage of communication development the child is currently at. In *10 Minutes for Talking*, I separate early communication skills into four stages.

Stage 1: Infant Talk (Not yet using words) p. 9
Stage 2: Baby Talk (Beginning to use words) p. 28
Stage 3: Toddler Talk (Using short phrases/sentences) p. 49
Stage 4: Preschooler Talk (Conversational) p. 70

Just by reading the titles of the stages, you probably have a "gut instinct" for which stage your child is at. I suggest going to the stage that corresponds with your gut first. If you read that stage and find that the skills listed are more advanced than the communication your child uses, go one stage back. If, on the other hand, you find that your child is more advanced than you thought, go one stage forward.

It's easy to maximize your child's communication skills in less than 10 minutes a day when you focus on providing a language-rich environment throughout your child's daily activities! While there are more than 200 specific ideas to provide that language-rich environment in *10 Minutes for Talking*, it is my hope that these ideas help you see the infinite, natural opportunities available to you and your child that promote communication development and enrich your interactions.

Enjoy your interactions with your child and relax! Interaction that is fun and engaging is what will encourage your child to seek out more interactions. Follow your child's lead as you play and have fun!

All my best wishes as you communicate to the max with your child!

Amy Maschue

Amy Maschue, M.S. CCC-SLP
Certified Speech-Language Pathologist & Mom of 6

INFANT TALK

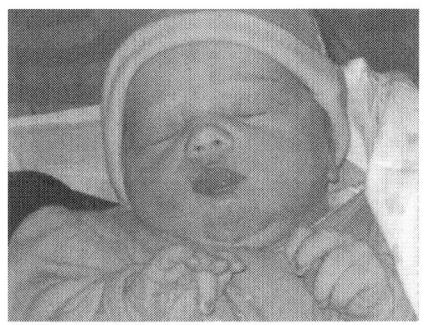

Maximize Your Child's Communication Potential

The First Year

INFANT TALK: HOW INFANTS COMMUNICATE
(Not Yet Using Words)

There's nothing like looking at the face of a sweet infant and holding him in your arms. It is one of the most peaceful and joyful activities I can think of. We are born to communicate. You are probably not aware what a natural communicator your newborn is. Your infant has been sharing information with you since day one! Many parents, especially Dads, (sorry Dads) think all newborns do is eat, sleep and poop. While it certainly feels that way in the early months, infants actually begin vocalizing with the first cry. I'll bet you never realized you'd been participating in "baby dialogues" all this time! When I point this fact out, I often get asked, "Which communication skills should my infant be using?"

In general, infants communicate by crying, vocalizing (i.e., cooing which is making vowel sounds for example "ahhhh" or babbling which is making consonant and vowel non-words for example "bama"), watching and looking, and gesturing. They typically communicate to express their needs and wants as well as to take social turns. You will often see an infant make "raspberry" or other noises back-and-forth with you or a sibling and smile and laugh in between each turn. You will notice an infant instinctively put everything to his mouth to explore and learn. The bumpy, knubby ball feels hard, but good on teething gums, while the soft, chewy stuffed toy feels good to rub on the face. I remember fondly with each of my kids, enjoying the back-and-forth of sound play during diaper changes. I loved the coos and gurgles my infants made as I sang to them, smiled and gave butterfly kisses after taking care of their dirty diapers. The cute infant laugh after a blow on the belly always made my day!

All of this experiential knowledge the infant gains through his senses builds a foundation for organizing and understanding the world around him as well as attempting to express his own ideas, needs and wants related to people and objects in his daily life. When you watch an infant it's easy to see that he is far from passive in communication. On the contrary, an infant is soaking up every piece of communication information given. Infants "know" two main rules about communication with others:

Rule #1: "I DO something to GET something."
- Cry to get fed.
- Smile to be held.
- Shake a toy to make noise.

Rule #2: "I learn through my senses."
- Put everything in mouth to explore.
- Watch things and people carefully.

In one short year, these rules allow an infant to make huge communication gains. He changes from communicating through cries and purposeful noises to understanding simple commands (e.g., "Give mommy the ball.") and attempting to use 2-3 words besides "mama" and "dada" to express his needs and wants (PRO-ED, 1999). Amazing!

HOW TO USE 10 MINUTES FOR TALKING WITH YOUR INFANT

Step 1: Get to Know How Your Child Communicates

On page 13, you will find a general overview of the way infants communicate in the first year to help you identify how your infant is using his face, sounds, words and knowledge about the world to communicate with you. On page 14, you will find a more detailed checklist of communications skills a child should acquire by approximately 12 months of age. Remember, this checklist is only a guide. There is a huge range of typical development. I suggest that you read each skill listed and note:

1. Which skills your child has acquired (i.e., consistently uses independently) by writing a "+" next to the corresponding skill.

2. Which communication skills are at your child's "Growing Edge"? These are the skills that are next in line for your child to acquire. (These are also the skills that the *10 Minutes for Talking* activities will help to develop more quickly and consequently help your child communicate to the MAX!)

Completing this checklist will give you a quick picture of how your child currently communicates and which communication skills will be next to develop. The increased awareness you gain from completing this checklist about your child's communication skills is invaluable, as your expectations for communication set the bar for your child's participation in conversation. I suggest you revisit this checklist at least every three months and marvel at the gains your child has made.

Step 2: Maximize Communication in Less than 10 Minutes Starting TODAY!

On pages 15-25, you'll find five specific suggestions for each of the typical activities children participate in everyday: getting dressed, brushing hair and teeth, meal preparation, sharing meals, bath time, playing on his own, playing with other children, playing with an adult, riding in the car, shopping at the store, and bed time. I suggest choosing one suggestion within a single daily activity to implement at the beginning (e.g., during the morning routine sing songs to your infant as he looks at you while exaggerating your facial expressions). As you get comfortable implementing one suggestion you can add another to that same daily activity (e.g., after making exaggerated facial expressions for your infant to watch, you can imitate his facial expressions and noises) or choose to implement a suggestion from a different daily activity (e.g., use the sign for "eat" to describe what you are doing as you share a meal with your infant).

An easy way to remind yourself or any other caregiver or sibling which suggestion you are implementing is to make a copy of the page corresponding to the daily activity and hang it up in the room in which that activity occurs (e.g., morning routine page can be copied and taped up next to your child's bed). I like to use a bright highlighter to mark which suggestion we are currently implementing. It makes it easy for everyone who is interacting with your child to work together to maximize all opportunities to communicate!

From Crying to Conversation
How Infants Communicate: Birth to 1 yr

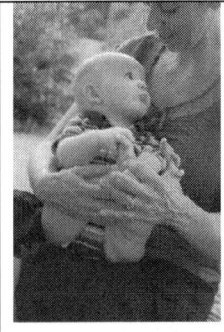	Infants use their face to communicate by... • Maintaining eye contact for 1-3 minutes • Alternating eye contact between people and objects • Imitating facial expressions with/without sounds, like: Sticking out tongue Moving lips (e.g., round/spreading) Opening and closing jaw Smiling, frowning, pouting Making "raspberry" sounds
	Infants use sounds, words and signs to communicate by... • Using gestures, like: Pointing and/or reaching Conventional gestures (e.g., waving hi/bye) Giving or showing objects to people Object-based actions (e.g., pushing a ball) Non-object-based actions (e.g., hand movements to songs) • Sequencing sounds Cooing (i.e., vowel sounds, like "ah" or "oh") Babbling (i.e., combining consonants and vowels, like "tata") Jargon (i.e., nonsensical strings of syllables) • Making sounds by approx 12 mos Initial-"word" position: b, d, h, g, m Final-"word" position: m • Attempting to say simple words (e.g., mama, ball, etc.) • Enjoying music and movement (e.g., Itsy Bitsy Spider, etc.)
	Infants share their knowledge about the world by... • Playing anticipation games (e.g., peek-a-boo, etc.) • Enjoying physical play (e.g., tickles, "Tummy Time," etc.) • Enjoying mirror exploration • Responding to name and recognizing the names of others • Tracking objects and attempting to explore with senses (e.g., watching mobiles/objects, putting toys in mouth, etc.)

From Crying to Conversation Checklist
Developmental Milestones for Communication, Speech and Language

The First Year: Birth to 1 yr

	Communication, Speech and Language Milestones
	Pre-Verbal Infants
	0-3 months
	Makes eye contact
	Cries
	Smiles
	Laughs
	Grunts
	Makes raspberry/spit sounds
	Coos (makes long "vowel-like" sounds)
	4-5 months
	Babbles (makes "consonant-like" sounds)
	Vocalizes to toys
	Responds to name
	6-9 months **(Great time to start modeling signs!)**
	"Echoes" or imitates sounds made by others
	Recognizes some words based on daily events
	Uses jargon (long strings of babble w/intonation)
	10-12 months
	Uses gestures to communicate
	•Conventional (e.g., yes, no, hi, bye)
	•Pointing
	•Giving/showing
	•Reaching (with and without contact)
	•Object-based actions ("See what I did", uses objects to do something in an interaction, e.g., rolling ball to another person)
	•Non-object-based actions (e.g., clapping, hand motions to a song)
	Initiates interaction with "first" words—uses familiar words like "mama" "dada" and other common nouns or action words (e.g., "up")
	Recognizes his/her name
	Understands simple instructions

Adapted from PRO-ED (1999) and Bleile (1995). Parents, keep in mind that the purpose of the above checklist is to provide general communication, speech and language milestones and a guide for typical acquisition ages; however, there is a generous range of acquisition for these skills that is still considered typical.

INFANT TALK

Morning Routine/Getting Dressed

The morning rush can be a natural time to facilitate language skills for several reasons: (a) it happens everyday, (b) younger children can learn from older children and (c) there is one-on-one interaction with an adult. Try these suggestions for maximizing the communication potential of your infant during your morning routine.

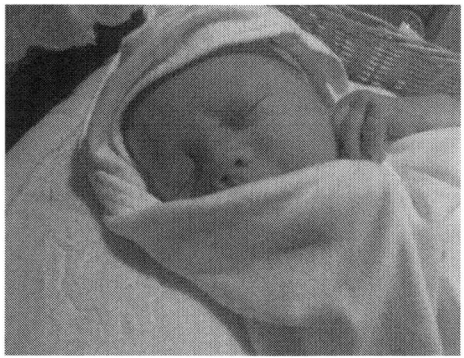

1. Sing songs to your child as he looks at you. Make your facial expressions bigger than life. It's easier for infants to notice exaggerated differences.

2. Imitate facial expressions and sounds your child makes. This activity is called "sound play" and facilitates the acquisition of speech sounds.

3. Label your child's body parts and describe what you are doing (e.g., "arm in" as you put his arm in the onsie).

4. Play "peek-a-boo" while you change his clothes.

5. Listen to soothing music as you massage your child as you change him—if at least 6 months old using the hand-over-hand method to help your child request "more" massage.

INFANT TALK

Brushing Hair and Teeth

Brushing hair and teeth can be stressful activities because some children are sensitive to the feel of the brushes. Associating brushing activities with "fun", social time with a parent/caregiver can actually make brushing hair and teeth a fun, language-learning activity. The earlier you start the better! Try these suggestions for maximizing the communication potential of your infant during your brushing routine.

1. Hold your child so that he faces you at eye-level as you gently brush his hair. Smile and say soothing things in a calm, low voice (e.g., I'm brushing your soft hair, It feels good to brush hair, etc.). Even let your infant have a turn brushing your hair when he is able to hold the brush.

2. Do the same as above with a "Nuk" brush or infant toothbrush on the inside of his cheeks and tongue. This activity stimulates the nerve endings in the mouth and will encourage vocalizations and mouth "games" (e.g., raspberries, lip popping/smacking, etc.).

3. Sing a silly song about brushing your teeth while you brush your child's teeth (e.g., You brush your teeth, Cha Cha Cha Cha Cha Cha Cha Cha Cha Cha).

4. Make silly faces in the mirror while your infant looks into it. Exaggerate motions with your eyes as you brush your child's hair/teeth.

5. Describe what you're doing as you brush your child's hair/teeth (e.g., "I'm brushing your brown hair. Your hair is so soft."). This activity facilitates advanced grammatical forms and increases vocabulary.

INFANT TALK

During Meal Preparation

Keeping kids busy and out of harm's way during meal preparation can be a challenge. It seems that meal prep time is precisely when kids need you to attend to a variety of "emergencies". Keeping the kids in the kitchen area where they can be watched and involving them in meal preparation to a degree can make this time less stressful while promoting communication and language skills. Try these suggestions for maximizing the communication potential of your infant when you are preparing meals.

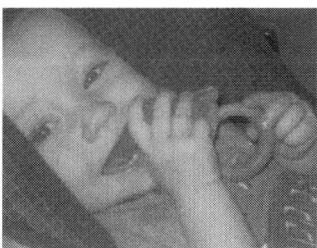

1. Put your child in a safe seat (e.g., high chair, swing, megasaucer, etc.) and let them watch you make food. If old enough, use one of the food introduction mesh bags to let your infant taste as he watches without risk of choking.

2. Describe what you're making and talk about the sounds, smell, color and taste of cooking. This is your chance to be your own Food Network Star!

3. Give your child a spoon and unbreakable pot or bowl and let them explore the noises they can make.

4. Designate a drawer in your kitchen that has child-friendly cooking objects to play with. Talk about the objects, their function and sounds they make.

5. Let your child play with pretend food (e.g., plastic play food). Label the food and actions (e.g., cutting, biting, and stirring).

INFANT TALK

At Mealtime

Mealtime has traditionally been a time that family members gather and share about their days. By focusing on promoting language and communication development with the entire family, you can encourage the other family members to become more involved in communication activities. Try these suggestions for maximizing the communication potential of your infant during mealtime.

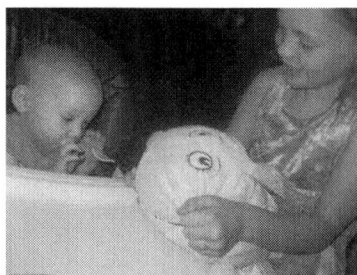

1. Describe what your child is doing (e.g., "eat", "drink").

2. Use signs to encourage requesting (e.g., "eat", "more"). Model the signs approximately three times for every time you help your infant make the sign (Hand-Over-Hand) or request a vocalization.

3. Play food games to get your child's mouth open (e.g., airplane).

4. Use a soft spoon to "wipe" inside of your child's cheeks. Smile and talk about how it feels to "stretch" and label the body parts (e.g., "lips", "cheeks"). The result is an increase in sensory information to your infant's mouth that will make him more vocal and interested in exploring orally.

5. Make funny faces after taking a bite and encourage your child to copy you. Label the faces with a corresponding emotion (e.g., happy face-smile, sad face-frown, mad face-furrowed brow, surprised face-"O" lips and big eyes).

INFANT TALK

At Bath time

Bath time is a great place to facilitate language skills because most children enjoy water play. Whether you are having a quick or playtime bath, it is easy to talk about how the water feels, label body parts or to pretend your child is a dirty shark swimming in the ocean. For children who do not like bath time, language activities can make it fun---or at least distract their attention and provide a good opportunity for them to "use their words" to tell you what they don't like about the bath. Try these suggestions for maximizing the communication potential of your infant during bath time.

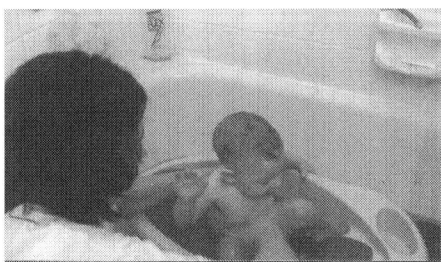

1. Sing a song related to washing/water. "It's raining it's pouring", "I am washing", "Scrub a dub".

2. Label your child's body parts as you wash them.

3. Make and maintain eye contact with a smile as you wash your child calmly.

4. Use bath toys to hide under a washrag. Once your child recognizes the "hiding" routine, change it by putting the wash rag in front, floating in the water, while hiding the toy behind him.

5. Play peek-a-boo body parts with a towel or washrag. This activity allows you to get body parts clean while you teach. Talk about soft scrubbing, water temperature and washing speed (e.g., fast between toes, slow on arm) to introduce and/or compare and contrast vocabulary and concepts.

INFANT TALK

While Playing on His Own

Being able to play alone is an important skill for children of all ages. When your child plays alone it gives him opportunities to practice the different skills he has been exposed to throughout the day and learn to keep himself busy. This time also allows you to watch what your child is doing on his own. You may be surprised at what your child "got" out of different actions. Try these suggestions for maximizing the communication potential of your infant while he plays on his own.

HELPFUL HINT: Keep a few toys out of the toy rotation so that if you need your child to play by himself there is a "new" really interesting toy to keep his attention.

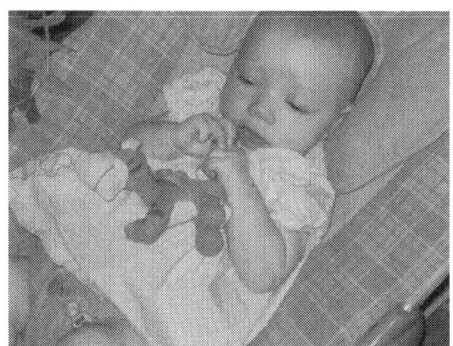

1. Turn on a mobile in your child's crib.

2. Put a child-safe mirror near the changing table, crib/bed.

3. Put child on tummy with 2-3 visually-interesting rattles/toys.

4. Use a "kick-and-play" toy.

5. Make a sheet of pictures of family members' faces—laminate it so that your child can drool and chew on it.

INFANT TALK

While Playing with Other Children

Children are very good teachers for each other. They enjoy playing together and they present communication opportunities that adults would not think to provide due to (a) their creativity and (b) their own communication skill limits. Try these suggestions for maximizing the communication potential of your infant while he plays with other children.

Typically, when a child is nonverbal he primarily participates in "solitary" or "parallel" play (i.e., he prefers to play by himself or next to another child). This type of play is developmentally appropriate. The following suggestions are for helping older children interact with nonverbal children. The older child practices his communication skills while the younger child benefits from the real-life communication scenario.

1. Have the older child make funny faces for your infant to enjoy.

2. Let the older child hold a rattle or other visually-interesting toy at your infant's eyelevel and play "keep away".

3. Have the older child tell a story with props (e.g., Barbies, stuffed animals) to your infant.

4. Help the older child play peek-a-boo with your infant.

5. Have the older child sing a song to your infant with finger motions.

INFANT TALK

During Playtime with an Adult

Time spent with you is very special time to your child. Keep in mind the following guidelines: (1) to get consistent eye contact with your child you need to bring him up to your level or get down on his, (2) keep energy in your voice, use correct grammar and sound production, and (3) follow your child's lead, play with the toys he is interested in. Try these suggestions for maximizing the communication potential of your infant during playtime with adults.

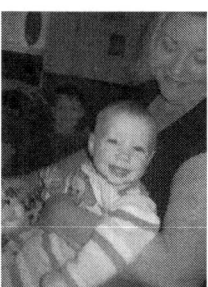

1. Dance with your child-be sure to be at his eyelevel. This can be a great quad workout for you!

2. Model high frequency signs (e.g., more, up, my turn, eat) while playing with the child's favorite toy.

3. Respond to any of your child's facial expressions with enthusiasm in order to encourage your child to increase the number of turns he takes in an interaction.

4. Blow bubbles and wait for your child to "ask" for more—this may be in the form of eye contact, reaching for the bubbles in your hand, smiling, a sign, or a word approximation.

5. Pat the ground in a simple beat pattern when your child looks at you. Repeat each time your child makes eye contact. You'll love his attempts to copy you.

INFANT TALK

While on a Car Ride

Car time can be stressful. There are many activities that you can prepare ahead of time that will promote language development while keeping your child busy in the car. I suggest putting together a bag of "car toys". I include actual toys, the markers that only write on the special paper, puppets and books. These toys stay in the car. I do not suggest using videos to keep your infant busy except on rare occasions, such as a particularly long car trip. Try these suggestions for maximizing the communication potential of your infant while loading and riding in the car.

1. Smile and say soothing things as you load your child in the car seat.

2. Sing a song as you carry your child to his car seat. This activity will build a routine and help him anticipate the expectations for getting in the car.

3. Listen to your child's favorite music on the ride.

4. Put a child-safe mirror in the back seat with your child and describe their face as you drive (You need not see their face for obvious safety reasons, but you can say things like "Look at your big, blue eyes" or "Who's that cute baby?").

5. Put pictures of family members on sticky tape or Velcro and stick them to the back seat for your child to look at. Talk about the people in the pictures.

INFANT TALK

While in the Store

If you have more than one child, then you have likely experienced the "tantrum on aisle 7". It seems that children, no matter how old, sense that our attention is distracted and see store visits as a time to practice communication breakdowns. The key to a low stress store visit is to set a routine/ground rules early on. Be mindful that your child will likely ask (or grab for) things EVERY time you go to the store. Just a warning-Buying him something regularly seems like no big deal when he simply wants a cracker pack, but it's a hard pattern to break. Try these suggestions for maximizing the communication potential of your infant while in the store.

1. Bring a set of toys to keep your child engaged. Talk about what he is doing with the toy (e.g., "You are chewing on Elmo's foot."). You can rotate toys at home to keep the toys your child already owns "new".
2. Give your child an object to look for while in the cart (e.g., a big store mascot, logo, etc.). Talk about where it might be, colors to look for, and don't forget to make bigger than life faces to keep him engaged while "looking" (e.g., "Let's look for the big red circle. Oh...I see something red!").
3. Sing songs with hand motions and touch games. If you are singing and he is participating, he'll stay in the cart.
4. Bring snacks to keep your child busy in the cart. Keep the snacks in your pocket and let him "ask" for more. If you allow him to practice his requesting with signs or word approximations while controlling the snack handout rate, you can make one snack pack last the entire store visit.
5. "Wear" your infant in a face-forward position in your wrap, sling or "kid" backpack. This will allow him to be looking out at the interesting people in the aisles and see all the goods as you walk by them. (This is my infant's favorite activity at the store!).

INFANT TALK

During the Bedtime Routine

Routines are very important to children. They like patterns and they thrive in predictable situations. There are many different philosophies regarding the bedtime ritual. In terms of using the bedtime routine to facilitate language development, there are many communication opportunities available because things are typically calm and quiet. It also tends to be a time that your child gets some one-on-one time with you. Having the same activities occur at bedtime each night can create the predictability that children like and promote language development. Try these suggestions for maximizing the communication potential of your infant while getting him ready for bed.

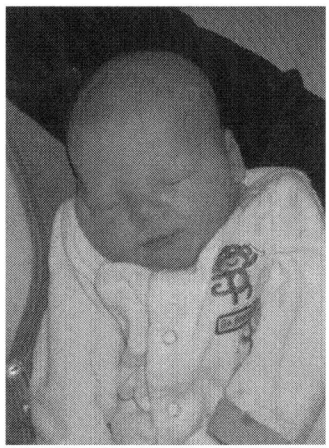

1. Hum or sing a song.

2. Read a picture book. You can even, hand-over-hand, help your infant touch the pictures as you read.

3. Give your child a body massage as you talk softly about the day.

4. Kiss and label each body part good night.

5. Talk about how fun it is to put on pajamas. Make up a silly rhyme/song and play peek-a-boo as you dress your child.

INFANT TALK

Using Sign to Facilitate Communication

American Sign Language (ASL) is an actual language. However, when using signs with a child for the purpose of facilitating language development, use of official ASL signs is not necessary.

Teaching signs to young children has been demonstrated to facilitate communication skills because it is the visual representation of words and is motorically easier to produce than spoken words (Hegde, 1996). I recommend that parents and caregivers begin modeling 5-10 simple signs relevant to your child's daily activities at approximately six months of age. Signs should be general and motorically-basic (e.g., more, my turn, open, eat, drink, play, ball, dog, cat, Mommy, Daddy, up). It is suggested to model the signs as well as help the child perform the signs using your hands to guide his motor execution of the sign (called Hand-over-Hand production). For example, you can help him use the sign for "my turn" (i.e., tapping his hand over his heart), then give him a turn with a fun toy.

I am often asked about how to "get rid" of the signs once the child begins to talk. The signs naturally decrease in use because words are quicker and more effective as they are understood by familiar AND unfamiliar communication partners. Signs typically drop when the child gets a 50-100 spoken word vocabulary.

Using signs really maximizes the communication potential of your infant because the motor system of a child under age 12 months typically cannot sequence the motor plan to produce words as the primary mode of communication. The learning of signs as an infant will continue to have benefits in your child's language development as a preschooler. As a child who used signs early, your child was an early pattern detector AND producer. Pattern detection and production is a base skill in reading, writing and spelling. Amazing what connections made in these early years can do isn't it!

Here's my 3 year-old demonstrating some of the early signs we use in our home.

BABY TALK

Maximize Your Child's Communication Potential

The Second Year

BABY TALK: HOW BABIES COMMUNICATE
(1-Word User/New Talker)

Your baby begins his journey to toddlerhood with his first word attempts. Be warned of two things. First, words are like a light switch permanently stuck in the "on" position; once he starts talking, he won't stop (think of the Why question phase). Second, his babyhood goes by quickly, so enjoy it! The early baby dialogues you've shared with your infant, the coos and giggles, are sweet, but the next part of the journey is just as fun.

In general, babies communicate much like infants with the addition of more and more frequent attempts to communicate with single words. Remember, these single words will likely NOT sound like the adult productions. This is the fun stage where your baby will use the limited sound inventory he has to talk about any and all ideas. The result of the mismatch between your baby's speech motor skills and growing expressive vocabulary is completely normal and even cute. Your baby will use word approximations like "uh" for "up" or "tat" for "cat". These sound errors are part of typical development and will be replaced with more and more adult-like productions as his second year goes by.

In this stage, your baby will still need to use crying, cooing (i.e., strings of nonsensical vowel sounds like, ah eh oh) and babbling (i.e., strings of nonsensical sounds that contain consonants and vowels, like babamaguh) to communicate as he is still working with a relatively limited number of speech motor skills and vocabulary. He will be watching EVERYTHING and soaking up information like a sponge. You should notice that your baby increases his attempts to communicate and when taking his communication turn may make a series of somewhat unintelligible sounds that you swear is a sentence (aka "jargon")! Babyhood is my favorite stage from a speech and language standpoint. I loved watching my babies hold up a toy and use their jargon to "tell" me all about the truck or dolly they were holding. As they ended this year of development, it got even better.

My favorite "baby talk" story happened with my daughter Jillian, then 19 months old. We were in the process of buying a new car because I was pregnant with Maeve and we needed another seat. It had been a long day of test driving for my husband and I and a long day of sitting in the car for the kids. Jillian had enough of her brother's pestering and hit Tommy. My husband told Jillian to say sorry to Tommy. Jillian said nothing. My husband pulled over the car, turned around and said, "Jillian, you hurt Tommy. We are not going anywhere until you say sorry to Tommy." Jillian stared at him with a blank expression and said nothing. My husband waited a moment, and then said in a stern voice, "Jillian say sorry!" Jillian looked straight at her Daddy and said with all seriousness, "I can't talk." The whole car busted out laughing! (We did compose ourselves and wait to leave until Jillian said sorry to Tommy a few moments later.)

Just as he did in his infanthood, your baby will typically communicate to express his needs and wants as well as to take social turns. Now though, your baby will communicate with an increased frequency, efficiency and effectiveness. As an infant he "knew" two main rules about communication with others:

Rule #1: "I DO something to GET something."
- Cry to get fed.
- Smile to be held.
- Shake a toy to make noise.

Rule #2: "I learn through my senses."
- Put everything in mouth to explore.
- Watch things and people carefully.

Now, your baby has added a third rule. He "knows":

Rule #3: "Words Work."
- Words are the most effective, efficient way to get things done.

This is when the magic world of words opens up to your baby! The first 5-10 words come in slowly, but once he establishes the rule "Words Work," watch out (typically at approximately 25-50 words in the child's expressive vocabulary). In the second year of life, your baby will have moved from "beginning to try" to use words to express ideas, need and wants to producing more than 300 words (PRO-ED, 1999)!

HOW TO USE 10 MINUTES FOR TALKING WITH YOUR BABY

Step 1: Get to Know How Your Child Communicates
On page 33, you will find a general overview of the way babies communicate in the second year to help you identify how your baby is using his face, sounds, words and knowledge about the world to communicate with you. On page 34, you will find a more detailed checklist of communications skills a child should acquire by approximately 24 months of age. Remember, this checklist is only a guide. There is a huge range of typical development. I suggest that you read each skill listed and note:

>   1. Which skills your child has acquired (i.e., consistently uses independently) by writing a "+" next to the corresponding skill.
>
>   2. Which communication skills are at your child's "Growing Edge"? These are the skills that are next in line for your child to acquire. (These are also the skills that the *10 Minutes for Talking* activities will help to develop more quickly and consequently help your child communicate to the MAX!)

Completing this checklist will give you a quick picture of how your child currently communicates and which communication skills will be next to develop. The increased awareness you gain from completing this checklist about your child's communication skills is invaluable, as your expectations for communication set the bar for your child's participation in conversation. I suggest you revisit this checklist at least every three months and marvel at the gains your child has made.

Step 2: Maximize Communication in Less than 10 Minutes Starting TODAY!
On pages 35-45, you'll find five specific suggestions for each of the typical activities children participate in everyday: getting dressed, brushing hair and teeth, meal preparation, sharing meals, bath time, playing on his own, playing with other children, playing with an adult, riding in the car, shopping at the store, and bed time. I suggest choosing one suggestion within a single daily activity to implement at the beginning (e.g., during the morning routine leave out the last word in each phrase of a familiar song

for your child to fill in). As you get comfortable implementing one suggestion you can add another to that same daily activity (e.g., lay out your child's clothes in order and ask him to label each item) or choose to implement a suggestion from a different daily activity (e.g., while making lunch, hide the pretzels under your child's napkin and then quickly take the napkin off for your child to label the food).

An easy way to remind yourself or any other caregiver or sibling which suggestion you are implementing is to make a copy of the page corresponding to the daily activity and hang it up in the room in which that activity occurs (e.g., morning routine page can be copied and taped up next to your child's bed). I like to use a bright highlighter to mark which suggestion we are currently implementing. It makes it easy for everyone who is interacting with your child to work together to maximize all opportunities to communicate!

Remember, this checklist is only a guide: there is a huge range of typical development. I provide this checklist so that you can note:

> 1. Which skills your child has acquired (i.e., consistently uses independently) by writing a "+" next to the corresponding skill.
>
> 2. Which communication skills are at your child's "Growing Edge"? These are the skills that are next in line for your child to acquire. These are also the skills that the *10 Minutes for Talking* activities will help to develop more quickly and consequently help your child communicate to the MAX!

From Crying to Conversation
How Babies Communicate: 1 yr to 2 yrs

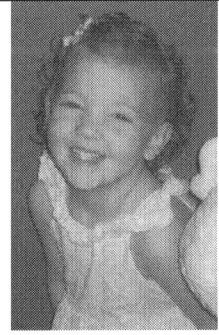	Babies use their face to communicate by... • Alternating eye contact between people and objects for at least two conversational turns • Imitating facial expressions with/without sounds, like: Sticking out tongue Making extreme lip movements (e.g., round/spreading lips) Opening and closing jaw Smiling, frowning, pouting Making "raspberry" sounds
	Babies use sounds, words and signs to communicate by... • Using gestures/words at a rate of at least 1/minute, like: Pointing and/or reaching Conventional gestures (e.g., waving hi/bye) Giving or showing objects to people Object-based actions (e.g., pushing a ball) Non-object-based actions (e.g., hand movements to songs) Words (can be approximations) • Speaking with improving intelligibility Is 25% intelligible in conversation by 18 mos Is 75% intelligible in conversation by 24 mos • Using more words and attempting to combine words in conversation, songs, rhymes, etc. "Says" 10-20 words by 18 mos "Says" 300 words by 24 mos Uses simple phrases (e.g., "no go") by 2 yrs Enjoys music-tries to fill-in words/motions Refers to self by name
	Babies share their knowledge about the world by... • Playing early pretend (e.g., imitation of adults) and carrying on conversations with self and dolls • Recognizing pictures of familiar objects and people • Following simple commands • Distinguishing print from non-print • Understanding simple questions and commands

From Crying to Conversation Checklist

Developmental Milestones for Communication, Speech and Language

The Second Year: 1 yr to 2 yrs

Communication, Speech and Language Milestones
Single-Word Talkers
By 1 ½ Years
Uses 10-20 words
25% intelligible
Recognizes pictures of familiar people/objects
Begins to combines two-words like "no go" or "blue ball"
Uses words to make wants known (e.g., "up")
Points and gestures to all attention to an event and to show wants
Follows simple commands
Imitates simple actions
Hums, may sing simple tunes
Distinguishes print from non-print
Early Multi-Word Talkers
By 2 Years
Uses approximately 300 words
Knows how to interact with books (holds correctly)
50-75% intelligible
Stays with one activity for 6-7 minutes
Asks for food and drink
Forms some plurals by adding "s"
Uses two word negative phrases, such as "no dog"
Names pictures
Refers to self by name
Uses sentence length of 2-3 words
Asks "What" and "Where" (not grammatically correct—e.g., "What this?" or "Where baby?"
Carries on conversations with self and dolls (not completely intelligible or grammatically correct, but "sounds" like a conversation)
Identifies body parts on self and others
Understands simple questions and commands

Adapted from PRO-ED (1999) and Bleile (1995). Parents, keep in mind that the purpose of the above checklist is to provide general communication, speech and language milestones and a guide for typical acquisition ages; however, there is a generous range of acquisition for these skills that is still considered typical.

BABY TALK

Morning Routine/Getting Dressed

The morning rush can be a natural time to facilitate language skills for several reasons: (a) it happens everyday, (b) younger children can learn from older children and (c) there is one-on-one interaction with an adult. Try these suggestions for maximizing the communication potential of your baby during your morning routine.

1. Leave out the last word in a familiar song about body parts (e.g., sing Head, Shoulders, Knees and Toes and let your child fill in the word "toes" and "nose").

2. Lay out your child's clothes in order and ask your child to label the items.

3. Ask your child which clothing item goes on first (e.g., "What goes first, socks or shoes?").

4. Tickle each body part as your child "helps" you put on his clothes.

5. Ask your child which clothing item goes on each body part (e.g., Where should we put your shirt? On your legs or your arms?).

BABY TALK

Brushing Hair and Teeth

Brushing hair and teeth can be stressful activities because some children are sensitive to the feel of the brushes. Associating brushing activities with "fun", social time with a parent/caregiver can actually make brushing hair and teeth a fun, language-learning activity. The earlier you start the better! Try these suggestions for maximizing the communication potential of your baby during your brushing routine.

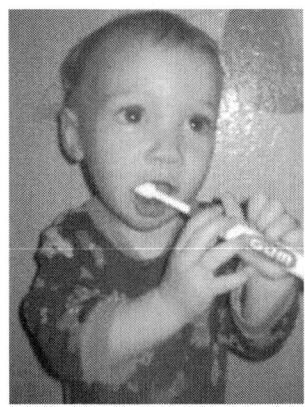

1. Allow your child to brush your hair/teeth-let them have fun as you describe how it feels and why it is important.

2. Let your child fill in words to fun songs you sing about brushing (e.g., to the tune of "Mary Had a Little Lamb" sing, "Everybody brush your teeth, brush your teeth, brush your teeth. Everybody brush your teeth and smile all day long.").

3. Let your child choose which brush/comb or hair accessories you use (e.g., Which brush do you want to use: little or big?).

4. Count as you brush your child's teeth/hair. This will give him a more concrete concept of time.

5. Give your child a toy and a brush to brush the toy's hair/teeth while you brush his.

BABY TALK

During Meal Preparation

Keeping kids busy and out of harm's way during meal preparation can be a challenge. It seems that meal prep time is precisely when you're needed to attend to a variety of "emergencies". Keeping the kids in the kitchen area where they can be watched and involving them in meal preparation to a degree can make this time less stressful while promoting communication and language skills. Try these suggestions for maximizing the communication potential of your baby when you are preparing meals.

1. Hide some food you are preparing under a paper towel. Take off the paper towel quickly. Ask your child to name the food.

2. Pretend you're going to cut the food with a spoon as a "joke". This activity is fun because it takes advantage of his knowledge of routine. Kids LOVE when you change the routine as a "joke".

3. Encourage your child to copy the actions you do with pretend or unbreakable kitchen objects (e.g., stir when you stir, etc.).

4. Hold up a utensil. Ask your child to show you what to do with it (e.g., hold up a spoon and say, "Spoon. What do you do with a spoon?"—do with unfamiliar objects like potato mashers).

5. Ask your child to tell you "how to cook" (e.g., hold up a spoon, "Should I cut or stir?").

BABY TALK

At Mealtime

Mealtime has traditionally been a time that family members gather and share about their days. By focusing on promoting language and communication development with the entire family, you can encourage the other family members to become more involved in communication activities. Try these suggestions for maximizing the communication potential of your baby during mealtime.

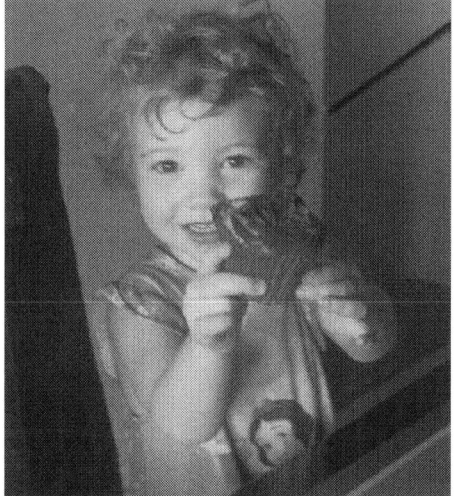

1. Continue to use signs with words to promote requesting for "eat" and "drink". The signs will naturally extinguish on their own as he becomes a better talker.

2. Begin to model 2-word phrases by describing what you are eating/drinking (e.g., "drink milk", "poke food").

3. Play "copy cat" food games. Get your child to take a bite then you take bite. They can be "big bites", "small bites", etc.

4. Model some words that describe the food as you eat it (e.g., crunchy, slimy). Ask your child to tell you what he would call it.

5. Label the food your child is eating as he puts it in his mouth.

BABY TALK

At Bath time

Bath time is a great place to facilitate language skills because most children enjoy water play. Whether you are having a quick or playtime bath, it is easy to talk about how the water feels, label body parts or to pretend your child is a dirty shark swimming in the ocean. For children who do not like bath time, language activities can make it fun---or at least distract their attention and provide a good opportunity for them to "use their words" to tell you what they don't like about the bath. Try these suggestions for maximizing the communication potential of your baby during bath time.

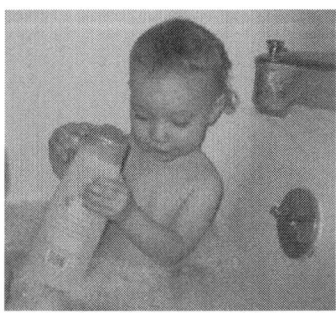

1. Blow bubbles in the water. Talk about how the bubbles change when you blow fast or slow.

2. Practice following simple directions like "kick", "splash", and "scrub".

3. Let your child tell you which body part to wash or give your child a choice (e.g., "Do you want me to wash your arm or leg?").

4. Talk about what the bath toys are doing (e.g., going up, down, hiding under, in/out of the water, jumping off the tub, etc.).

5. Give your child a washrag. Squeeze out the rag in your hands and say, "water down." Do it again in your hand and then in your child's. See if your child will begin to say "water down" or another 2-word phrase.

BABY TALK

While Playing on His Own

Being able to play alone is an important skill for children of all ages. When your child plays alone it gives him opportunities to practice the different skills he has been exposed to throughout the day and learn to keep himself busy. This time also allows you to watch what your child is doing on his own. You may be surprised at what your child "got" out of different activities. Try these suggestions for maximizing the communication potential of your baby while he plays on his own.

HELPFUL HINT: Keep a few toys out of the toy rotation so that if you need your child to play by himself there is a "new" really interesting toy to keep his attention.

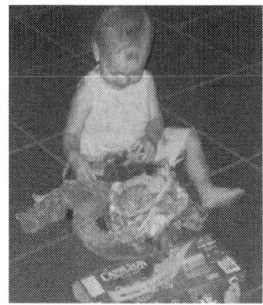

1. Provide your child with toys that require him to "do" something (e.g., touch a button, turn a lever, etc.) before it plays music or lights up.

2. Put out playscapes with related toys (e.g., barn with pigs, cows, chicken, farmer, tractor).

3. Give your child books to "read". You'll be surprised at the words you'll hear as he describes/reads to himself.

4. Play a short video that has lots of singing, movement and learning opportunities.

5. Set out brushes, pretend food, etc. and baby dolls or stuffed animals.

BABY TALK

While Playing with Other Children

Children are very good teachers for each other. They enjoy playing together and they present communication opportunities that adults would not think to provide due to (a) their creativity and (b) their own communication skill limits. Try these suggestions for maximizing the communication potential of your baby while he plays with other children. Typically, when a child is nonverbal he primarily participates in "solitary" or "parallel" play (i.e., he prefers to play by him/herself or next to another child). This type of play is developmentally appropriate. As a baby, your child should be moving from a preference for parallel play to interactive play. The following suggestions are for helping other children interact with babies.

1. Have the children sit across from one another and roll a ball back and forth. To encourage the children to ask each other for the ball by "using words" (e.g., "ball" or "my turn"). It's okay to use hand-over-hand sign if necessary.

2. Set up a "bowling alley" with plastic cups and use a ball to have the children play bowling. One child can set up, one can knock down, then they can switch roles

3. Play a CD with familiar children's songs and have the children dance to the music (e.g., Ring around the Rosey, Old MacDonald). Kids of all ages love "Freeze Dance".

4. Put out some 5-10 piece puzzles and have the children find the pieces for their own puzzle from a single pile placed between the kids.

5. Get out the stuffed animals and baby dolls and accessories. Encourage the kids to help each other take care of the toys.

BABY TALK

During Playtime with an Adult

Time spent with you is very special time to your child. Keep in mind the following guidelines: (1) to get consistent eye contact with your child you need to bring him up to your level or get down on his, (2) keep energy in your voice, use correct grammar and sound production, and (3) follow your child's lead, play with the toys he is interested in. Try these suggestions for maximizing the communication potential of your baby during playtime with adults.

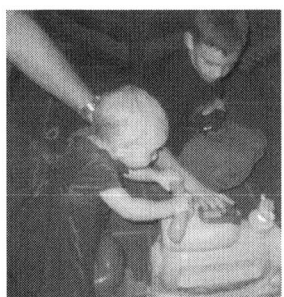

1. Put stuffed animals or other light weight toys (e.g., bean bags) in a basket and take turns dumping them out on each other's hands.

2. Make a "kid sandwich". Lay your child on your lap and pretend to put on mayo, meat, etc. Add in "crazy" foods like spaghetti and ask for your child's ideas.

3. Roll a ball back and forth using signs and words to request a turn.

4. Read a 5-10 page book with predictable lines (e.g., Spot books, Maisy, etc.). You may read it several times.

5. Take turns hiding under a blanket and making different funny faces when you take the blanket off your head.

BABY TALK

While on a Car Ride

Car time can be stressful. There are many activities that you can prepare ahead of time that will promote language development while keeping your child busy in the car. I suggest putting together a bag of "car toys". I include actual toys, the markers that only write on the special paper, puppets and books. These toys stay in the car. I do not suggest using videos to keep your baby busy except on rare occasions, such as a particularly long car trip. Try these suggestions for maximizing the communication potential of your baby while loading and riding in the car.

1. Describe what you are doing as you "click" your child into the car seat.

2. Pretend that you can't get the clips to go together and you need your child's "muscles" to help click them.

3. Sing a favorite song and leave the last word of each phrase out (e.g., "I'm a little __) or let your child pick an animal to sing a song about.

4. Describe where you are going in a First, Next, Last format.

5. Talk about who you are going to see and what you are going to do when you get there.

BABY TALK

While in the Store

If you have more than one child, then you have likely experienced the "tantrum on aisle 7". It seems that children, no matter how old, sense that our attention is distracted and see store visits as a time to practice communication breakdowns. The key to a low stress store visit is to set a routine/ground rules early on. Be mindful that your child will likely ask (or grab for) things EVERY time you go to the store. Just a warning-Buying him something regularly seems like no big deal when he simply wants a cracker pack, but it's a hard pattern to break. Try these suggestions for maximizing the communication potential of your baby while in the store.

1. Bring a set of toys to keep your child engaged. Talk about what he is doing with the toy (e.g., "Your baby is riding."). I suggest those toys be fun and relatively novel to keep his attention. (You can rotate toys at home to keep the toys your child already owns "new" to him).
2. Give your child an object to look for while in the cart (e.g., a big store mascot, logo, etc.). Talk about where it might be, colors to look for, and don't forget to make bigger than life faces to keep him engaged while "looking" (e.g., "Let's look for the big red circle. I see red!").
3. Sing songs with hand motions and touch games. If you are singing and he is participating, he'll stay in the cart.
4. Bring snacks to keep your child busy in the cart. Keep the snacks in your pocket and let him "ask" for more. If you allow him to practice his requesting with signs or word approximations while controlling the snack handout rate, you can make one snack pack last the entire store visit.
5. Put food items next to your child in the cart. Help him point to the details on the packages (e.g., "This is a can of green beans. Touch the Giant.").

BABY TALK

During the Bedtime Routine

Routines are very important to children. They like patterns and they thrive in predictable situations. There are many different philosophies regarding the bedtime ritual. In terms of using the bedtime routine to facilitate language development, there are many communication opportunities available because things are typically calm and quiet. It also tends to be a time that your child gets some one-on-one time with you. Having the same activities occur at bedtime each night can create the predictability that children like and promote language development. Try these suggestions for maximizing the communication potential of your baby while getting him ready for bed.

1. Read/tell your child his favorite story.

2. Talk about what you and your child did that day. Use chunking words (e.g., first, next, last) to help him recall the events of the day.

3. Sing a bedtime song together.

4. Help your child "tuck in" a stuffed animal to bed. Describe what they are doing.

5. Describe which body part is being put into his pajamas. Give him a choice regarding which body part goes in first.

BABY TALK

How to Maximize Communication by Facilitating Sound System Development

Your child's understanding of the world is changing by leaps and bounds in his second year of life. The more ideas about the world your child has, the more he has to communicate with others about. His sound system supports his vocabulary acquisition. Sounds are needed to produce words. As your child's expressive vocabulary grows more sounds are needed to talk about his needs and wants. In fact, there is actually a reorganization of your child's sound system due to his word learning that occurs throughout this year (Bleile, 1995).

You will witness this reorganization by noticing the increase in your child's overall attempts to say new words with established sounds (sounds he says correctly) as well as his attempts to say new, more complex sounds in words. In the beginning of the second year, your baby's expressive vocabulary will be influenced by two main "trues" of development. First, he will talk about concrete things in his immediate experiences. Second, he will select the words he attempts to produce based on the sound characteristics of the word (Bleile, 1995). He will use motorically simple sounds. Sounds like b, p, m, n, d, t, k and g that are produced by completely stopping the airflow, then allowing it to explode; they, along with vowels are the earliest sounds to develop. (The sounds made at the front of the mouth will develop earlier than those produced at the back of the throat.) He will produce these sounds in the context of more motorically simple syllable shapes. These syllable shapes are characterized by open (i.e., no consonant on the end of the word), repetitive syllable shapes (e.g., mama, dada). By the end of this year, you will see the addition of more complex sounds that require more motor control to produce a continuous flow of air (e.g., f, s, sh, etc.) and more complex syllable shapes that are closed (i.e., have a consonant on the end of the word) and more varied in shape (e.g., open, cup).

Because your baby's sound system plays such an important role in communication, here are a few suggestions to help you maximize the development of your child's sound system.

1. **Play with Sounds.**
While enjoying communication in any engaged activity, sound play is easy to do. It can be as simple as:

- Modeling words that start with the same sound (e.g., alliteration of "b" when you say "big baby belly" as you tickle his tummy during changing time).
- Using rhyming words (e.g., as you hold the ball up high between you and your baby say, "I've got the ball. Ball, tall, wall…fall", then let the ball fall in your baby's lap).

2. **Use Stress and Rhythm to Highlight Sounds and Syllable Shapes**
Throughout your daily interactions with your baby, you will undoubtedly use several different types of sounds and syllable shapes. He will be paying attention to all of them. You can highlight new or more complex sounds and syllable types by varying the stress and rhythm with which you say them. You can do this by:

- Singing familiar, repetitive songs and pausing to allow your baby to fill in the last word of each phrase (e.g., Twinkle, Twinkle, Little ___. How I wonder what you ___).
- Giving equal stress in your models of words with multiple syllables and/or complex sound structures (e.g., el-e-phant, ba-na-na, Jill-i-an).

3. **Provide visual, touch and auditory cues to help introduce new sounds and syllable shapes.**
Kids use different modalities to maximize their learning. Your baby learns by watching, hearing and doing. You can help him produce new and/or more complex sounds and syllables by providing cues that highlight different learning modalities. You can do this by:

- Tapping out the syllables on your or your baby's leg as you say a word.

- Gently gliding your fingers along your baby's forearm as you say words with "long" sounds (i.e., words that require continuous airflow like sip, snake, fish, sheep, sleep, etc.).
- Adding a short pause between the syllables of a word (e.g., "rabb"-pause-"it").
- Modeling a "prep" sound to highlight the sound's characteristics (e.g., making a "cough-like k" sound before modeling the word "cup" to highlight the place of articulation for the k, making a "ha-ha-ha" breathy sound before modeling the word "hide" to highlight the continuous airflow of the h, etc.).

Facilitating the development of your baby's sound system really maximizes the communication potential of your baby because the sound system supports word acquisition and production. Awareness of sounds and their characteristics alone and in words as a baby will continue to have benefits in your child's language development as a preschooler. Sounds have similarities and words are created by putting sounds together in a predictable way. As with the suggestion given in the infant section to use signs with your child to maximize communication, your use of the above sound system suggestions will help your child be an early pattern detector AND producer. Remember, pattern detection and production are base skills in reading, writing and spelling. Isn't it great how easy and fun it can be to give our children a leg up in skills that will truly impact their ability to communicate their ideas, needs and wants?

10 Minutes for Talking

TODDLER TALK

Maximize Your Child's Communication Potential

The Third Year

TODDLER TALK: HOW TODDLERS COMMUNICATE
(2-3 Word Phrases/"Telegraphic Talker")

Get ready for personality! I love the toddler stage. Your toddler will amaze and amuse you with his understanding of the world around him. In this stage, he's working towards conversation, but lacks grammatical sophistication and wholistic comprehension of the abstract nature of the world. He will be literal, but curious about the unknown. A classic example at this age occurs when a toddler tries to tell a joke. A simple "knock knock" joke brings roaring laughter from the toddler, while at the same time going completely over his head. When he tries to tell a joke, which he will insist on doing, his joke will showcase either (a) his literal bent (e.g., "Knock, knock. Who's there? Door. Door who?...Door ha, ha, ha!") or (b) his simple desire to participate and continue the dialogue by reverting to an "old standby" (e.g., "Knock, knock. Who's there? Poo Poo! Ha ha ha!").

This is the time in development when your toddler moves from a worldview dictated by his perspective alone to a worldview that acknowledges and is curious about the perspectives of others. Toddlers love talking about their favorite things. They also like hearing about what you like and why. Try having a conversation about favorite ice cream flavors or cartoon characters. You'll enjoy the back and forth nature of the conversation...so different than when your child was a baby! It will start to feel like a real conversation.

The more you converse with your toddler, the more you will see your toddler try to use language to assert his opinion and even try to convince others to join him. This skill is particularly impressive considering that a year ago your child was just learning to use single words. To see this new skill in action, ask your child to retell you a story or about an event that he knows well. He will have lots of important details to share. During the conversation, offer a differing opinion or account of the events. When your child realizes that your story doesn't jive with his story, be prepared for a long recounting of the story events, the character's costumes, etc. Your toddler will try to establish his expertise in the subject, and consequently the superiority of his version, by giving lots of details and lots of enthusiasm. While your toddler acknowledges you can both have different views, the insight stops there. He can't yet express in a logical and structured way WHY his view is different, and at least in his opinion, better than yours.

I found a classic example of this when looking through old videos of my children. When my third child Philip was two, he played pretty much everyday with his "best friend"/cousin Alli. (She is five weeks older than Philip.) Alli and Philip had a disagreement the day before. Alli hit Philip when he took her toy. The video taped conversation between Philip and I was detailed, but always on message: "Alli was mean. She hit me." The conversation went like this:

Philip (eating a granola bar): She just mean. And then she turned nice.
Mom: Well she's your best friend now.
Philip: Well she just turned back.
Mom: Back again to what?
Philip: Back. So mean like a monster! (Philip makes a monster face.)
Mom: What do you do when that happens?
Philip (back to eating): I kick her.
Mom: No you talk to her, right? Words work best.
Philip: I talk to her.
Mom: Say, "I'm sorry I took your toy, but I don't like when you hit me."
Philip: I telled her mom. She hit me.
Mom: Well that's a good idea to get help, but you did take her toy. I think you should both act nicely.
Philip: (long pause) and then she got in trouble. Alli hit me. (Philip laughs.) She likes me now. We're best friends.

In general, toddlers communicate by watching, looking, doing and talking. They typically communicate to express their needs and wants as well as to take social turns. Toddlers love predictability of routines, like songs they know, and will enjoy playing, singing and talking about the same ideas over and over again. You will see a definite set of favorite stories, foods, etc. develop. While your toddler will still be working with a speech and language system mismatch (i.e., he "knows" more than he has the speech motor and language skills to express), you will see a HUGE increase in:

- the number of words he can say.
- the complexity of his ideas.
- the length of his utterances (remember they will still contain speech sound and grammatical errors).
- the intelligibility of his conversational speech.

In fact, by the end of the third year, toddlers have an expressive vocabulary of approximately 1,000 words, use 3-4 word sentences with early grammatical forms like plural s (e.g., cats) and "ing" (e.g., jumping) and be 90-100% intelligible to unfamiliar listeners.

As a baby, your child "knew" three main rules about communication with others:

Rule #1: "I DO something to GET something."
- Cry to get fed.
- Smile to be held.
- Shake a toy to make noise.

Rule #2: "I learn through my senses."
- Put everything in mouth to explore.
- Watch things and people carefully.

Rule #3: "Words Work."
- Words are the most effective, efficient way to get things done.

Now, your toddler has added a fourth rule. He "knows":

Rule #4: "I think. You think."
- Different people see things differently.

In this third year, these rules allow a toddler to make gains in social language that were not possible as a younger child. He changes from communicating through single words and simple sentences to using his language to talk about events and people with greater detail than he had before (PRO-ED, 1999). Amazing!

HOW TO USE 10 MINUTES FOR TALKING WITH YOUR TODDLER

Step 1: Get to Know How Your Child Communicates
On page 55, you will find a general overview of the way toddlers communicate in the third year to help you identify how your toddler is using his face, sounds, words and knowledge about the world to communicate with you. On page 56, you will find a more detailed checklist of communications skills a child should acquire by approximately 36-42 months of age. Remember, this checklist is only a guide. There is a huge range of typical development. I suggest that you read each skill listed and note:

> 1. Which skills your child has acquired (i.e., consistently uses independently) by writing a "+" next to the corresponding skill.
>
> 2. Which communication skills are at your child's "Growing Edge"? These are the skills that are next in line for your child to acquire. (These are also the skills that the *10 Minutes for Talking* activities will help to develop more quickly and consequently help your child communicate to the MAX!)

Completing this checklist will give you a quick picture of how your child currently communicates and which communication skills will be next to develop. The increased awareness you gain from completing this checklist about your child's communication skills is invaluable, as your expectations for communication set the bar for your child's participation in conversation. I suggest you revisit this checklist at least every three months and marvel at the gains your child has made.

Step 2: Maximize Communication in Less than 10 Minutes Starting TODAY!
On pages 57-67, you'll find five specific suggestions for each of the typical activities children participate in everyday: getting dressed, brushing hair and teeth, meal preparation, sharing meals, bath time, playing on his own, playing with other children, playing with an adult, riding in the car, shopping at the store, and bed time. I suggest choosing one suggestion within a single daily activity to implement at the beginning (e.g., during the morning

routine give your child a choice between two clothing items). As you get comfortable implementing one suggestion you can add another to that same daily activity (e.g., keep all your child's shoes in one basket and have him pick out matches) or choose to implement a suggestion from a different daily activity (e.g., during bath time let your child use measuring cups to talk about more and less).

An easy way to remind yourself or any other caregiver or sibling which suggestion you are implementing is to make a copy of the page corresponding to the daily activity and hang it up in the room in which that activity occurs (e.g., morning routine page can be copied and taped up next to your child's bed). I like to use a bright highlighter to mark which suggestion we are currently implementing. It makes it easy for everyone who is interacting with your child to work together to maximize all opportunities to communicate!

From Crying to Conversation
How Toddlers Communicate: 2 yrs to 3 yrs

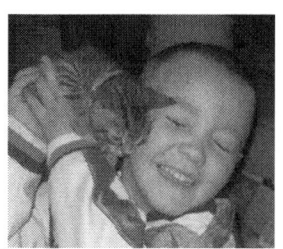	Toddlers use their face to communicate by... • Imitating adult-like nonverbal communication, body language and facial actions in play
	Toddlers use sounds, words and signs to communicate by... • Speaking with noticeably improving intelligibility Is 75% intelligible in conversation by 24 mos Is 90-100% intelligible in conversation by 36 mos • Using more words and attempting to combine words in conversation, songs, rhymes, etc. Says 300 words by 24 mos Says 1,000 words by 36 mos Producing 2-4 word sentences consistently (may not be grammatically correct)
	Toddlers share their knowledge about the world by... • Playing thematically • Identifying body parts, colors, shapes, etc. • Following multi-step commands • Distinguishing print from non-print • Knowing book routines • Knowing personal information and nursery rhymes

From Crying to Conversation Checklist
Developmental Milestones for Communication, Speech and Language

The Third Year: 2 yrs to 3 yrs

	Communication, Speech and Language Milestones
	Established Multi-Word Talkers: By 2 ½ Years
	Uses approximately 450 words
	Gives first name
	Uses past tense
	Uses plurals
	Combines some nouns and verbs
	Refers to self as "me" rather than name
	Tries to get adult attention with "watch me"
	Likes to hear same story repeated
	Uses "no" or "not" in speech
	Answers "where" questions
	Uses short sentences, such as "me do it"
	Holds up fingers to tell age
	Talks to other children and adults with success
	Plays with sounds of language
	Early Conversationalist: By 3 years
	Uses approximately 1,000 words
	90-100% intelligible
	Matches primary colors: names one color
	Knows day and night
	Begins to understand prepositional phrases, such as "put the block under the chair"
	Practices by talking to self
	Knows last name, gender, street name, and several nursery rhymes
	Tells a story or relays an idea has a sentence length of 3 to 4 words
	Consistently uses most sounds correctly
	Draws circle and vertical line
	Sings songs
	Stays with one activity for 8 to 9 minutes
	Asks "what" questions

Adapted from PRO-ED (1999) and Bleile (1995). Parents, keep in mind that the purpose of the above checklist is to provide general communication, speech and language milestones and a guide for typical acquisition ages; however, there is a generous range of acquisition for these skills that is still considered typical.

TODDLER TALK

Morning Routine/Getting Dressed

The morning rush can be a natural time to facilitate language skills for several reasons: (a) it happens everyday, (b) younger children can learn from older children and (c) there is one-on-one interaction with an adult. Try these suggestions for maximizing the communication potential of your toddler during your morning routine.

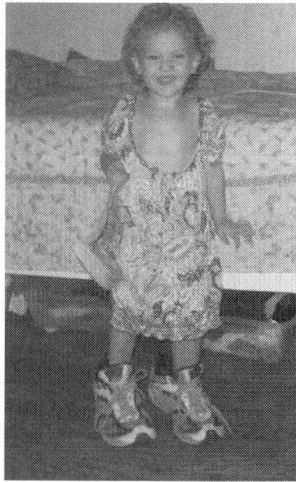

1. Have a "race" to put on each item of clothing. You can even set a timer with a beeper.

2. Give your child a choice between two shirts or shoes (e.g., "Do you want to wear the yellow shirt or the blue shirt?).

3. Keep all of your child's shoes in one drawer. Pick out one shoe and talk about what the shoe looks like. Ask your child to find the match.

4. Sing familiar songs and let your child fill in phrases of the song.

5. Play a funny faces game---After each arm, leg, foot, etc. is put in the appropriate clothing, make a funny face or say a funny phrase for your child to copy (e.g., "gottcha slippery leg").

TODDLER TALK

Brushing Hair and Teeth

Brushing hair and teeth can be stressful activities because some children are sensitive to the feel of the brushes. Associating brushing activities with "fun", social time with a parent/caregiver can actually make brushing hair and teeth a fun, language-learning activity. The earlier you start the better! Try these suggestions for maximizing the communication potential of your toddler during your brushing routine.

1. Make up a story about funny animals/aliens that have a special language you can learn to speak by talking with your toothbrush in your mouth—You could even draw pictures of the "aliens" and hang them on your bathroom mirror.

2. Buy your child a toothbrush or hairbrush with a favorite character on it. When brushing, talk about the character.

3. Use a sticker chart to reward your child's cooperation with the hygiene routine.

4. Turn on music and encourage your child to brush to the rhythm of the music.

5. Compete—how fast can we brush our hair/teeth.

TODDLER TALK

During Meal Preparation

Keeping kids busy engaged and out of harm's way during meal preparation can be a challenge. It seems that meal prep time is precisely when you're needed to attend to a variety of "emergencies". Keeping the kids in the kitchen area where they can be watched and involving them in meal preparation to a degree can make this time less stressful while promoting communication and language skills. Try these suggestions for maximizing the communication potential of your toddler when you are preparing meals.

1. Play utensil matching (i.e., get 2 forks, 2 spoons, 2 cups and put in a bag). Let your child pick a utensil from the bag and try to match it to the corresponding utensil laid in a row on the floor or at the table.

2. Have your child sort a snack that won't spoil dinner (e.g., cheerios, pretzels, grapes). Have your child separate the snacks into piles. Talk about how the piles are the same/different.

3. Help your child make-up a recipe. Try to make it later.

4. Ask your child to put the placemats/accessories on the table.

5. Tell your child how to make a simple 3-4 step recipe. Have him repeat it.

TODDLER TALK

At Mealtime

Mealtime has traditionally been a time that family members gather and share about their days. By focusing on promoting language and communication development with the entire family, you can encourage the other family members to become more involved in communication activities. Try these suggestions for maximizing the communication potential of your toddler during mealtime.

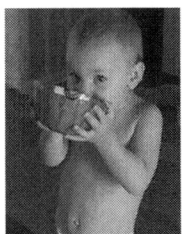

1. Use carrier phrases (i.e., phrases in which only the last word changes) to talk about your favorite food in the meal. Each person at the table could say, "I like ___.".

2. Make up funny 2-3 word "names" for the food in the meal (e.g., "crazy carrots", "green worms" for green beans). Talk about the noise the food might make if it could talk.

3. Have your child tell another adult or older child at the table what they had fun doing today.

4. Ask your child to tell you what food to take a bite of next.

5. Ask your child if they remember what they ate at a previous meal.

TODDLER TALK

At Bath time

Bath time is a great place to facilitate language skills because most children enjoy water play. Whether you are having a quick or playtime bath, it is easy to talk about how the water feels, label body parts or to pretend your child is a dirty shark swimming in the ocean. For children who do not like bath time, language activities can make it fun---or at least distract their attention and provide a good opportunity for them to "use their words" to tell you what they don't like about the bath. Try these suggestions for maximizing the communication potential of your toddler during bath time.

1. Make bubble bath faces (e.g., bubble beard).

2. Pretend to "clean" the tub while taking a bath. Talk about the different sponges, scrubbing hard, etc.

3. Bring measuring cups and spoons into the tub and talk about who has the "most" and the "least" water.

4. Let your child watch as the water goes down the drain. Talk about what it looks and sounds like and where the water goes.

5. Let your child experience "hot" and "cold" water.

TODDLER TALK

While Playing on His Own

Being able to play alone is an important skill for children of all ages. When your child plays alone it gives him opportunities to practice the different skills he has been exposed to throughout the day and learn to keep himself busy. This time also allows you to watch what your child is doing on his own. You may be surprised at what your child "got" out of different actions. Try these suggestions for maximizing the communication potential of your toddler while he plays on his own.

HELPFUL HINT: Keep a few toys out of the toy rotation so that if you need your child to play by himself there is a "new" really interesting toy to keep his attention.

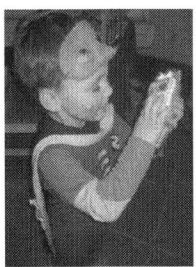

1. Make puzzles available with pieces your child can easily pick up and manipulate.

2. Encourage your child to build things with legos/blocks.

3. Color pictures from coloring books or make pictures on blank paper.

4. Get out musical instruments (or pots and pans) and ask your child to practice a "concert" that he can perform for the family later.

5. Put out matching games for your child to play.

TODDLER TALK

While Playing with Other Children

Children are very good teachers for each other. They enjoy playing together and they present communication opportunities that adults would not think to provide due to (a) their creativity and (b) their own communication skill limits. Try these suggestions for maximizing the communication potential of your toddler while he plays with other children.

1. Allow the children to pick a picture from a coloring book and share crayons by asking one another for crayons using the names of the colors (e.g., "blue crayon").

2. Encourage sharing by helping the children to "use their words" by modeling a carrier phrase that they can imitate to request a turn (e.g., "I want ___." "My turn for ___.").

3. Turn on music and dance crazy together—you can turn the music off and play freeze or make up dances.

4. Get out musical instruments and have the children practice a concert to play for you later.

5. Get out a train set/playhouse and the related toys. Encourage the children to play out "real life" situations (e.g., Daddy going to work, etc.).

TODDLER TALK

During Playtime with an Adult

Time spent with you is very special time to your child. Keep in mind the following guidelines: (1) to get consistent eye contact with your child you need to bring him up to your level or get down on his, (2) keep energy in your voice, use correct grammar and sound production, and (3) follow your child's lead, play with the toys he is interested in. Try these suggestions for maximizing the communication potential of your toddler during playtime with adults.

1. Read a familiar story (e.g., Goldilocks). Get out costumes, use pretend voices and ask your child to act out the story with you.

2. Pretend you are a farmer or bus driver with the pretend toys your child has. Make a road on the floor and pick up different animals/people.

3. Pretend you are a horse and your child needs a ride on your back. Have your child ask for a "fast", "slow", or "bumpy ride."

4. Have a tea party.

5. Get a favorite coloring book and color together. Talk about the colors, what part of the picture you want to color, etc.

TODDLER TALK

While on a Car Ride

Car time can be stressful. There are many activities that you can prepare ahead of time that will promote language development while keeping your child busy in the car. I suggest putting together a bag of "car toys". I include actual toys, the markers that only write on the special paper, puppets and books. These toys stay in the car. I do not suggest using videos to keep your baby busy except on rare occasions, such as a particularly long car trip. Try these suggestions for maximizing the communication potential of your toddler while loading and ridinging the car.

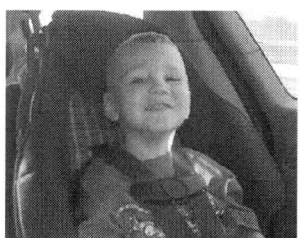

1. Turn on the radio or CD and have a family sing-a-long.

2. Have a "race" to see who can get into the car first. You can even "bet" who will make it in first.

3. Let your child bring puppets into the car and put on a puppet show in the back seat.

4. Play "I Spy" with the things you can see from the car window.

5. Discuss why you have seat belts, airbags, lights, brakes, a steering wheel, etc. in the car.

TODDLER TALK

While in the Store

If you have more than one child, then you have likely experienced the "tantrum on aisle 7". It seems that children, no matter how old, sense that our attention is distracted and see store visits as a time to practice communication breakdowns. The key to a low stress store visit is to set a routine/ground rules early on. Be mindful that your child will likely ask (or grab for) things EVERY time you go to the store. Just a warning: Buying him something regularly seems like no big deal when he simply wants a cracker pack, but it's a hard pattern to break. Try these suggestions for maximizing the communication potential of your toddler while in the store.

1. Bring a set of toys to keep your child engaged. Talk about what he is doing with the toy (e.g., "You are having your doll sit nicely in the cart."). I suggest those toys be fun and relatively novel to keep his attention. (You can rotate toys at home to keep the toys your child already owns "new" to him).
2. Give your toddler an object to look for while in the cart (e.g., a big store mascot, logo, etc.). Talk about where it might be, colors to look for, and don't forget to make bigger than life faces to keep him engaged while "looking" (e.g., "Let's look for the big red circle. Oh...I see something red!").
3. Put food items next to your child in the cart. Help him point to the details on the packages (e.g., "This is a can of green beans. Touch the Giant.").
4. Make your child a "list" of items to look for by using a crayon to circle needed items on the store circular.
5. Let him "drive" in the cart. Make a pretend "map" to follow on a scrap piece of paper from your purse and give the "play by play" to describe his "driving".

TODDLER TALK

During the Bedtime Routine

Routines are very important to children. They like patterns and they thrive in predictable situations. There are many different philosophies regarding the bedtime ritual. In terms of using the bedtime routine to facilitate language development, there are many communication opportunities available because things are typically calm and quiet. It also tends to be a time that your child gets some one-on-one time with you. Having the same activities occur at bedtime each night can create the predictability that children like and promote language development. Try these suggestions for maximizing the communication potential of your toddler while getting him ready for bed.

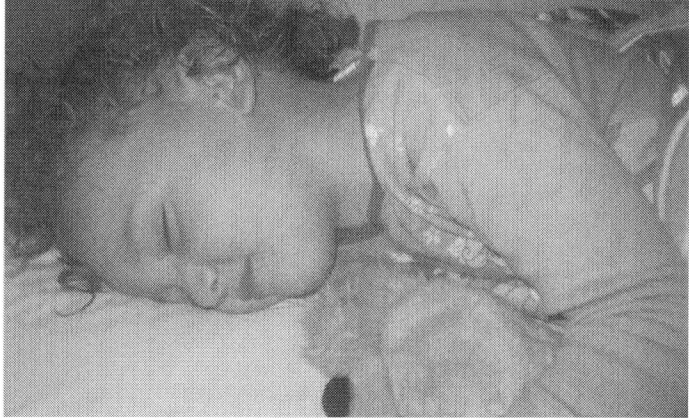

1. Read/tell your child his favorite story. Have him tell you what will happen on the "next page".

2. Have your child tell you the favorite thing he did that day.

3. Talk about animals that sleep at night and those that sleep in the day.

4. Discuss the fun things you will do together the next day.

5. "Check" that your child has all he needs for bed (e.g., ask your child if he has his pillow, covers, toy, etc.).

TODDLER TALK

How to Maximize Communication by Facilitating Grammatical Development

Your child's speech and language skills have progressed at an amazing and never-again-to-be-matched rate in his first three years. He's gone from a nonverbal communicator to a toddler on the verge of real conversations in a very short time. The transition from toddler to preschooler is often somewhat vague with regards to a concrete chronological age. Describing a child's communicative competence in conversation, for me as a SLP, is a much more functional milestone. To make the move from a telegraphic talker to a true conversationalist, your toddler needs to solidify his knowledge and use of grammatical patterns. Yes, once again, it's all about pattern detection and production!

There are special grammatical structures that research in child language development has found to mark the sufficient acquisition of the grammatical patterns for appropriate conversational skills in English by young children (Brown, 1973). These structures are called grammatical morphemes and essentially, they are pieces of grammatical information that change the meaning of the word they are associated with in a significant way. You can easily facilitate your toddler's acquisition of these grammatical morphemes by modeling them in your own conversation. Here are some suggestions for modeling these important grammatical structures.

1. **Talk about what people and things are doing and what they did**. Changes in verb tense (e.g., I am jumping, I jumped) are very important in English grammar. As your toddler is solidifying his understanding of verb tenses you will notice him try to over-generalize patterns he has learned (e.g., "I *jumped* on the pillow"-He learned that you add "ed" on the end of the verb to talk about things in the past-He applies to all verbs-"I *eated* the cracker."). Because being a successful communicator is all about being a good pattern detector and producer, stand tall and be proud of your toddler's hypothesis-testing abilities. To correct his over-generalization of the learned pattern, simply model back to him the correct pattern during the context of your conversation (e.g., "Yep. You *ate* all the

crackers. I think you *ate* all the peanutbutter too!"). Use your voice to add emphasis on the word that highlights the correct pattern (e.g., "*ate*") and model other words that demonstrate the patterns correctly applied (e.g., "You *drank* all the water too! That's ok, I *wrote* down crackers and peanutbutter on the grocery list. Wow we *snacked* on yummy food!").

2. **Talk about the location of people and objects.** Describing the location of people or objects to a point of reference is a great way to increase the length and complexity of your child's conversational language. If he can talk about where one object is in relation to another, he is giving his communication partner information that is specific and likely to be both effective and efficient in communicating his intended message (e.g., "I want the book" vs. "I want the book on the table.").

3. **Be aware of the grammatical details.** The little grammatical details that your toddler is learning in this third year of life are the details that once produced correctly and consistently will finalize his move from a telegraphic talker to a true conversationalist. When you are talking, you are modeling all the grammatical details correctly. However, as I described above, your toddler is busy detecting and trying out new grammatical patterns. To complicate matters, in English there are many exceptions to the rules. You may notice your toddler misuse pronouns (e.g., "Him is running." instead of "He is running."), leave out helper verbs (e.g., "I going to the pool." instead of "I'm going to the pool" or "I am going to the pool."), have difficulty using articles to specify objects (e.g., "I want an apple"—any apple vs. "I want the apple."---a specific apple), or incorrectly use third-person verbs (e.g., "He have candy." instead of "He has candy."). During this third year, these types of grammatical errors are developmentally normal. Continue to model the correct grammatical production and use your voice and multiple models to highlight the correct pattern for your child.

Your awareness of these growing edge grammatical skills will help you provide the language-rich environment best suited for maximizing your child's communication potential.

PRESCHOOLER TALK

Maximize Your Child's Communication Potential

The Fourth Year

PRESCHOOLER TALK: HOW PRESCHOOLERS COMMUNICATE
(Sentences/"Conversationalist")

Ever asked a preschooler what they think about ice cream, playing in the sprinklers or a favorite superhero? Likely, his answer was full of fantasy and detail. This language stage is marked by filibuster-like conversations. You ask a question and your child starts talking and talking and talking. As you enjoy these conversations with your preschooler, you probably also notice that the dialogue can lack direction: topics can change without warning, too much or too little detail may be given, sometimes the question posed isn't answered, etc. I love asking a preschooler to tell me about a favorite movie, TV show or book. They get so into the characters! Details about what the main characters were wearing, what they said, etc. abound. Then, a sibling or another child comes in with a new toy and without warning, we are off to another topic (e.g., That is the coolest toy. I always wanted that toy. That toy has green wings and can make noises when you push the buttons. My toys don't make noise anymore because my mom doesn't give them new batteries because she says they are too loud...).

In general, preschoolers communicate by watching, asking and talking in full sentences. As they did in earlier years, preschoolers communicate to express their needs and wants, but now the speech motor and language systems are beginning to catch up to the complexity of the preschooler's thoughts about the world. A preschooler can tell you what he wants and why! The introduction of causal statements (e.g., "I want the pink juice because pink is my favorite color."), and more complex grammatical structures like, embedded phrases (e.g., "I need the book *that I picked out* from the library."), conditional statements (e.g., "I'll get in the car *if* I can bring my dolls."), and time marking words (e.g., "*First*, we are eating dinner, *then* eating dessert, and *then* reading a story."), allow the preschooler to express needs and wants in an effective way that can also often work to negotiate or assert his opinion/desires.

Preschoolers also use their language to socialize and develop relationships. As toddlers, socialization was typically directed at communicating simple play ideas to peers and attempting more complex sharing with adults. Now, you'll notice your preschooler branching out socially. Play will become more dramatic and complex rather than thematic and imitation based. For example, while holding a purse and phone, a toddler might imitate things he has heard, "Hi honey. OK. Bye." A preschooler on the other hand, will talk as if he is really on the phone. Conversations might include topics like what he is doing right now, picking up the "big kids" at school or going to the movies or the store. The preschooler is dramatic. He assumes a role and now has the language skills to express variations of that role. He is also more fully able to play that role while interacting with another person. You won't believe how creative your preschooler will get!

Our first two children, Tommy and Annie are a year and a half apart and as such, have been close buddies since day one. When Tommy was three, we welcomed Philip into our family. I was a busy Mommy. Thank goodness Tommy and Annie had each other. One of my favorite memories of that crazy time is watching Tommy direct Annie while playing "Nemo". Tommy would get them both the most colorful blankets he could find to hold over their heads as they searched for their lost fish friend. Tommy ran throughout the house. Each room had a different danger or friend to meet: a whirlpool and turtle friend in the bedroom, a shark on patrol in the dining room, etc. Tommy introduced Annie to each "friend" and used three-step commands to tell her how they could avoid danger (e.g., First we can hide under this rock (aka table). Next, we can wait for the shark to swim away. Last, we can keep swimming!). It was so much fun to watch the two kids play together and listen to Tommy's imagination soar! (A great benefit to maximizing Tommy's language was that his skills pushed Annie's growing edge in everyday play. With all the great peer modeling, Annie's imagination and language skills weren't too far behind Tommy's.)

Another significant function of language that comes on line in the preschool years is that children move from using language for expression of needs/wants and simple social functions to using language to learn. Not only will a preschooler incessantly ask "Why," they will try to make connections between events, actions and causality. You will get many questions about how things work or requesting circumstantial details. A great example of this is conversing with a preschooler about events like his first birthday or when he was born. Kids of all ages love hearing about themselves, but if you pull out the baby book and share stories about the pictures, you will be amazed at the dialogues that ensue. Your preschooler will ask about, remember and retell details about your stories: What Mommy said to Daddy when you held him the first time, how he pooped on his uncle or spit up banana the first time he ate food. Now your preschooler's communicating for the shear enjoyment of sharing and learning information with others. Savor this stage. Write down the funny stories or insights your preschooler shares. They will be moments you forever treasure!

As a toddler, your child "knew" four main rules about communication with others:

Rule #1: "I DO something to GET something."
- Cry to get fed.
- Smile to be held.
- Shake a toy to make noise.

Rule #2: "I learn through my senses."
- Put everything in mouth to explore.
- Watch things and people carefully.

Rule #3: "Words Work."
- Words are the most effective, efficient way to get things done.

Rule #4: "I think. You think."
- Different people see things differently.

Now, your preschooler has added a fifth rule. He "knows":

Rule #5: "Our thoughts RELATE to each other."
- Ideas about the world exist in relation to one another. What I say/do effects what others say/do.

In this fourth year, these rules allow a preschooler to expand his vocabulary and comprehension by leaps and bounds, with sentences 5-6 words in length and use of complex grammatical structures (PRO-ED, 1999). Amazing!

HOW TO USE 10 MINUTES FOR TALKING WITH YOUR PRESCHOOLER

Step 1: Get to Know How Your Child Communicates
On page 76, you will find a general overview of the way preschoolers communicate in the fourth year to help you identify how your preschooler is using his face, sounds, words and knowledge about the world to communicate with you. On page 77, you will find a more detailed checklist of communications skills a child should acquire by approximately 48-60 months of age. Remember, this checklist is only a guide. There is a huge range of typical development. I suggest that you read each skill listed and note:

> 1. Which skills your child has acquired (i.e., consistently uses independently) by writing a "+" next to the corresponding skill.
>
> 2. Which communication skills are at your child's "Growing Edge"? These are the skills that are next in line for your child to acquire. (These are also the skills that the *10 Minutes for Talking* activities will help to develop more quickly and consequently help your child communicate to the MAX!)

Completing this checklist will give you a quick picture of how your child currently communicates and which communication skills will be next to develop. The increased awareness you gain from completing this checklist about your child's communication skills is invaluable, as your expectations for communication set the bar for your child's participation in conversation. I suggest you revisit this checklist at least every three months and marvel at the gains your child has made.

Step 2: Maximize Communication in Less than 10 Minutes Starting TODAY!
On pages 78-88, you'll find five specific suggestions for each of the typical activities children participate in everyday: getting dressed, brushing hair and teeth, meal preparation, sharing meals, bath time, playing on his own, playing with other children, playing with an adult, riding in the car, shopping at the store, and bed time. I suggest choosing one suggestion within a single daily

activity to implement at the beginning (e.g., during the morning routine use a star chart to help your child be more independent- talk about how to earn a star). As you get comfortable implementing one suggestion you can add another to that same daily activity (e.g., ask your child to describe what a sibling is wearing) or choose to implement a suggestion from a different daily activity (e.g., while on a car ride make up "knock knock" jokes).

An easy way to remind yourself or any other caregiver or sibling which suggestion you are implementing is to make a copy of the page corresponding to the daily activity and hang it up in the room in which that activity occurs (e.g., morning routine page can be copied and taped up next to your child's bed). I like to use a bright highlighter to mark which suggestion we are currently implementing. It makes it easy for everyone who is interacting with your child to work together to maximize all opportunities to communicate!

From Crying to Conversation
How Preschoolers Communicate: 4 yrs to 5 yrs

	Preschoolers use their face to communicate by... • Interpreting and using adult-like nonverbal communication, body language and facial actions in conversation
	Preschoolers use sounds, words and signs to communicate by... • Being 100% intelligible in conversation (may still have trouble saying s, r, l or th) • Saying > 2,000 words • Producing 4-6 word sentences consistently (typically grammatically correct) • Using the following grammatical structures: Plural s Prepositions (e.g., in, on, etc.) "Wh" questions (e.g., What, Who, When, Why) Negation (e.g., no, not) Past tense ed (e.g., ed as in "jumped') Irregular past tense (e.g., swam) To be verbs (e.g., is, am, are, was, were) • Enjoying music and movement (e.g., Itsy Bitsy Spider, etc.), filling-in and changing the words to "be silly" • Telling simple "stories" about personal events • Referring to self with pronouns (not always grammatically correct) • Questioning for information
	Preschoolers share their knowledge about the world by... • Playing dramatically • Identifying body parts, colors, shapes, etc. • Following multi-step (at least 3 step) commands • Distinguishing print from non-print • Knowing book routines, trying to "read" • Knowing personal information and nursery rhymes • Understanding same/different • Counting to 10 • Saying ABCs

From Crying to Conversation Checklist
Developmental Milestones for Communication, Speech and Language

The Fourth Year: 4 yrs to 5 yrs

Communication, Speech and Language Milestones
Established Conversationalist: By 4 Years
Points to red, blue, yellow and green
Identifies crosses, triangles, circles and squares
Knows "next month," "next year," and "noon"
Has sentence length of 4 to 5 words
Asks "who" and "why"
Begins to use complex sentences
Stays with activity for 11 to 12 minutes
Plays with language (e.g., word substitutions to joke)
Shows appreciation for and interest in print
Counts 10 objects
Sophisticated Conversationalist: By 5 Years
Uses approximately 2,000 words
Defines objects by their use and tells what they are made of
Knows address
Identifies penny, nickel and dime
Has sentence length of 5 to 6 words
Use speech sounds correctly, with exception of y, th, j, s/z, and r
Knows common opposites
Understands "same" and "different"
Uses future, present and past tenses
Stays with one activity for 12 to 13 minutes
Questions for information
Identifies left and right hand on self
Uses all types of sentences

Adapted from PRO-ED (1999) and Bleile (1995). Parents, keep in mind that the purpose of the above checklist is to provide general communication, speech and language milestones and a guide for typical acquisition ages; however, there is a generous range of acquisition for these skills that is still considered typical.

PRESCHOOLER TALK

Morning Routine/Getting Dressed

The morning rush can be a natural time to facilitate language skills for several reasons: (a) it happens everyday, (b) younger children can learn from older children and (c) there is one-on-one interaction with an adult. Try these suggestions for maximizing the communication potential of your preschooler during your morning routine.

1. Make a "star" chart for daily activities. As your child is dressing, talk about what you need to do to earn a star (e.g., put on your own shirt).

2. Ask your child to describe his favorite outfit or why he likes/dislikes what he is wearing today.

3. Ask your child to describe the clothes you or a sibling are/is wearing.

4. Talk about what you would wear if it was cold, hot, raining, etc. outside.

5. Name a clothing item and ask your child when he thinks you would need to wear it (e.g., snow boots, sunglasses, a hat, etc.).

PRESCHOOLER TALK

Brushing Hair and Teeth

Brushing hair and teeth can be stressful activities because some children are sensitive to the feel of the brushes. Associating brushing activities with "fun", social time with a parent/caregiver can actually make brushing hair and teeth a fun, language-learning activity. The earlier you start the better! Try these suggestions for maximizing the communication potential of your preschooler during your brushing routine.

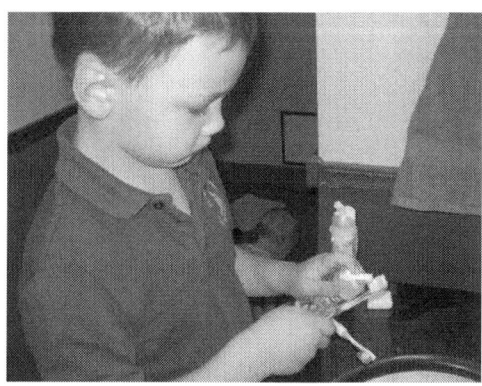

1. Let your child brush his own hair/teeth first, while you describe the steps (e.g., "First brush your bangs, then the back. Brush your hair to the side"). Then you can tidy up.

2. Have your child tell you the steps required to brush his hair/teeth.

3. Use a timer to challenge your child to brush his hair/teeth before the timer beeps.

4. Talk about the taste, color, texture, etc. of the toothpaste.

5. Discuss why you brush your teeth. Make up a story with the main characters "gingivitis" and "plaque". Your dentist might have some stickers or coloring pages.

PRESCHOOLER TALK

During Meal Preparation

Keeping kids busy engaged and out of harm's way during meal preparation can be a challenge. It seems that meal prep time is precisely when you need to attend to a variety of "emergencies". Keeping the kids in the kitchen area where they can be watched and involving them in meal preparation to a degree can make this time less stressful while promoting communication and language skills. Try these suggestions for maximizing the communication potential of your preschooler when you are preparing meals.

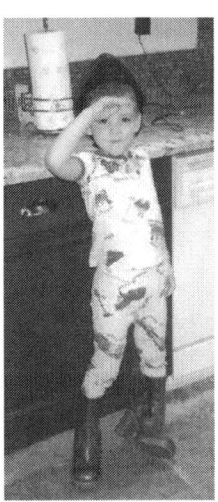

1. Have your child tell you about his favorite meal.

2. Ask your child to color a picture menu of the meal you are making.

3. Talk about the utensils, etc. required for the meal.

4. Have your child help you set a "formal" table (e.g., get bowls, salad plates, main course plates, regular spoon, soup spoon, etc.). Talk about what each piece is for.

5. Take a paper plate & separate it into at least three parts. Have your child draw in the food you are preparing by food group.

PRESCHOOLER TALK

At Mealtime

Mealtime has traditionally been a time that family members gather and share about their days. By focusing on promoting language and communication development with the entire family, you can encourage the other family members to become more involved in communication activities. Try these suggestions for maximizing the communication potential of your preschooler during mealtime.

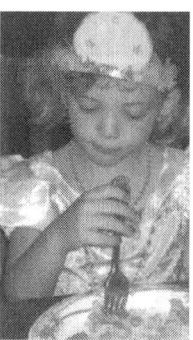

1. Talk about what you are eating at this meal. Discuss what other friends or kids in different places (e.g., grandma's house, birthday party) or other countries eat.

2. Take turns with your child describing what the food looks and tastes like.

3. Put food on your child's fork and feed it to them with their eyes closed. See if they can guess what it is.

4. Tell a story about mealtime when you were growing up. What did you like/dislike? Who did the cooking? Do you have a funny family story?

5. Share what everyone did that day or will do tomorrow.

PRESCHOOLER TALK

At Bath time

Bath time is a great place to facilitate language skills because most children enjoy water play. Whether you are having a quick or playtime bath, it is easy to talk about how the water feels, label body parts or to pretend your child is a dirty shark swimming in the ocean. For children who do not like bath time, language activities can make it fun---or at least distract their attention and provide a good opportunity for them to "use their words" to tell you what they don't like about the bath. Try these suggestions for maximizing the communication potential of your preschooler during bath time.

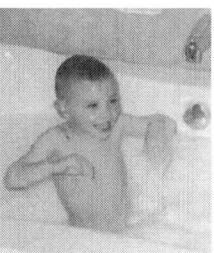

1. Pretend along with your child that you are a "sea creature". What noises would you make? What would you eat?

2. Talk about how each body part "got so dirty". Why are some parts cleaner than others (e.g., socks covering feet vs. hands)?

3. Splash in different ways-soft, hard, with your feet, with your hands.

4. Pretend your child is a scuba diver and "dive" for different toys.

5. Write on the tub walls with tub-safe crayons. Make pictures with your eyes closed. Have your child tell you what to draw, and then give your child a turn.

PRESCHOOLER TALK

While Playing on His Own

Being able to play alone is an important skill for children of all ages. When your child plays alone it gives him/her opportunities to practice the different skills he has been exposed to throughout the day and learn to keep himself busy. This time also allows you to watch what your child is doing on his own. You may be surprised at what your child "got" out of different actions. Try these suggestions for maximizing the communication potential of your preschooler while he plays on his own.

HELPFUL HINT: Keep a few toys out of the toy rotation so that if you need your child to play by himself there is a "new" really interesting toy to keep his attention.

1. Have your child "read" a book that he can talk to you about later.

2. Help your child set up a race track for car races or a train set for train play.

3. Let your child have some computer time.

4. Set out several puzzles and put all of the puzzle pieces in a pile. Have your child find where all the pieces go.

5. Get out dollhouses, pretend buses, etc. and let your child show his imagination.

PRESCHOOLER TALK

While Playing with Other Children

Children are very good teachers for each other. They enjoy playing together and they present communication opportunities that adults would not think to provide due to (a) their creativity and (b) their own communication skill limits. Try these suggestions for maximizing the communication potential of your preschooler while he plays with other children.

1. Get out the box of dress up clothes.

2. Get out the pretend food and have the children pretend to make a meal.

3. Have the child with the best language skills lead/sing songs to younger children.

4. Watch a movie together and then have the children act out the scenes.

5. Get out the play figures and related playscapes.

PRESCHOOLER TALK

During Playtime with an Adult

Time spent with you is very special time to your child. Keep in mind the following guidelines: (1) to get consistent eye contact with your child you need to bring him up to your level or get down on his, (2) keep energy in your voice, use correct grammar and sound production, and (3) follow your child's lead, play with the toys he is interested in. Try these suggestions for maximizing the communication potential of your preschooler during playtime with adults.

1. Read a book and then act out the story with toys, puppets, etc.

2. Read a familiar story and before you turn the page ask your child to tell you what will happen next.

3. While coloring, make up a first, next, last story up about the characters.

4. Get an old appliance or toy and have your child help you take it apart to see how it works.

5. Hide a toy behind your back and give your child three clues to see if he can guess what it is. Let him hide a toy and give clues as well.

PRESCHOOLER TALK

While on a Car Ride

Car time can be stressful. There are many activities that you can prepare ahead of time that will promote language development while keeping your child busy in the car. I suggest putting together a bag of "car toys". I include actual toys, the markers that only write on the special paper, puppets and books. These toys stay in the car. I do not suggest using videos to keep your baby busy except on rare occasions, such as a particularly long car trip. Try these suggestions for maximizing the communication potential of your preschooler while loading and riding in the car.

1. Describe in detail the route you are taking and then ask your child to repeat it back to you. If it's some place you go regularly, you could even draw a map together to help with directions.

2. Tell or make up "Knock Knock" jokes.

3. Label three things you see in the car and make up an adventure story that includes those three things.

4. Ask your child to tell how he think a car works. What does it "eat"? How does it "know" to turn?

5. Tell your child about the autopilot on an airplane and the cruise control in your car. Ask him how he thinks that works and talk about where your car would go if it got to pick the destination.

PRESCHOOLER TALK

While in the Store

If you have more than one child, then you have likely experienced the "tantrum on aisle 7". It seems that children, no matter how old, sense that our attention is distracted and see store visits as a time to practice communication breakdowns. The key to a low stress store visit is to set a routine/ground rules early on. Be mindful that your child will likely ask (or grab for) things EVERY time you go to the store. Just a warning: Buying him something regularly seems like no big deal when he simply wants a cracker pack, but it's a hard pattern to break. Try these suggestions for maximizing the communication potential of your preschooler while in the store.

1. Give your child a 2-3 step direction to point out items while in your line of site (e.g., "First show me the spaghetti sauce, then the noodles and last the cheese.").
2. Give your child an object to look for while in the cart (e.g., a big store mascot, logo, etc.). Talk about where it might be, colors to look for, and don't forget to make bigger than life faces to keep him engaged while "looking" (e.g., "Let's look for the big red circle. Oh...I see something red!").
3. Put food items next to your child in the cart. Help him point to the details on the packages (e.g., "This is a can of green beans. Touch the Giant.").
4. Make your child a "list" of items to look for by using a crayon to circle needed items on the store circular.
5. Let him "drive" in the cart. Make a pretend "map" to follow on a scrap piece of paper from your purse and give the "play by play" to describe his "driving".

PRESCHOOLER TALK

During the Bedtime Routine

Routines are very important to children. They like patterns and they thrive in predictable situations. There are many different philosophies regarding the bedtime ritual. In terms of using the bedtime routine to facilitate language development, there are many communication opportunities available because things are typically calm and quiet. It also tends to be a time that your child gets some one-on-one time with you. Having the same activities occur at bedtime each night can create the predictability that children like and promote language development. Try these suggestions for maximizing the communication potential of your preschooler while getting him ready for bed.

1. Read/tell you child his favorite story. Have him help you make up a new ending/tell what happened after the story was over.

2. Have your child tell three things he did that day. Use the words first, next and last to help your child chunk information and give more complete details.

3. Talk about how it feels good to get in your bed at the end of the day. Ask your child to tell you about what he likes best about bedtime.

4. Ask your child if he has ever had a dream. Tell him about a dream you had. Ask him what he will dream about tonight.

5. Make a "sweet dreams book". Draw a picture of the day's activities or good dreams from the night before.

PRESCHOOLER TALK

How to Maximize Communication by Facilitating the Development of Dramatic Play

Have you ever listened to two preschoolers play dolls or superheroes? If you have, you probably smiled when you heard amazing dialogues come out of these little people's mouths; words and phrases you never thought four-year-olds knew! You may have even heard reflections of your own conversations with your spouse or friends in the play of the children. Dramatic play helps your preschooler understand the power of language! During dramatic play your preschooler has the opportunity to react to another spontaneously and in real time, organize the play and make connections between actions and language that may be much advanced of his own skills (e.g., while playing checker at the "grocery store" set up in the kitchen, your preschooler may scan more items than his friend wants to purchase, the friend might say I don't want to buy that and a completely unique conversation can ensue).

Dramatic play is central to your child's learning and development in the preschool years (Piaget, 1962). When he plays, your preschooler can break through the restrictions of reality and pretend he is someone or something different from himself. When he does this, he deepens his understanding of the world, especially as it relates to and affects him and the people around him. In order to engage in dramatic play with another, your preschooler must explain who he is and what he is doing as well as get that same information from the others he is interacting with. He also has to choose language that fits the role. Because of this, dramatic play is an amazing way to practice perspective-taking skills and provides a learning opportunity for empathy and language related to more abstract concepts and emotions.

Now, don't think "Dramatic play...I've got to run out to the store, buy every costume on the shelf, set up a dramatic play area in the living room and buy every accessory for every conceivable play theme!". On the contrary. It's easy to maximize your child's communication skills through dramatic play, stay on a budget and not overwhelm your house with toys. I suggest having a prop box or basket filled with items that will spark your child's imagination.

Here's what I have in the dress-up box at our house.

- **Cardboard box blocks to build houses, make "roads", etc.**
- **Hats, old fancy shoes, ties, old Halloween costumes**
- **Old cell phones and purses**
- **Pretend food, pots and utensils**
- **Stuffed animals, superheroes and dolls, strollers, cradle**
- **Blankets and sheets for costumes and forts**
- **Cars and other vehicles**

What it comes down to is anything can be used to facilitate dramatic play. The sillier the better!

HOW BOOKS MAXIMIZE COMMUNICATION NOW AND IN THE FUTURE

You may find it hard to believe, but your child began his journey to literacy as an infant! Every interaction with you and others allows your child to pick up important information and language that will provide the building blocks for reading, writing and spelling. Even in the first year, you will find that your infant likes to look at pictures of people and objects. During the second year of life, you will find that your baby is enjoying the pictures, but also seeming to understand that you talk/"read" a book as evidenced by his jibber-jabber as he "reads" the book he holds upside-down. In the third year, your toddler is able to notice information about the pictures and the sounds of the words spoken while reading/looking at the book. Your preschool-age child will be excited to learn to read and often eager to tell you a story as he studies the pictures in a book.

Books offer a fun and extremely valuable opportunity for you to develop skills that will maximize the communication potential of your child now and on into his future. In 2008 the National Early Literacy Panel (NELP, 2008) examined more than 500 research articles considered by literacy experts to provide insight into the skills and abilities that are linked to later outcomes in reading, writing and spelling. The data from these articles was included in a meta-analysis in order to produce a quantitative summary of the literature. This summary indicated that six literacy-related variables consistently predicted later literacy outcomes. Those six variables were children's:

1. **Alphabet Knowledge** (Knowing the names and sounds associated with printed letters)

2. **Phonological Awareness** (Hearing and playing with the sounds of language-for example, rhyming or alliteration)

3. **Rapid Automatic Naming** (Quickly listing a sequence of letters or digits)

4. **Rapid Naming of Sequences** (Quickly naming a sequence of repeating sets of pictures, colors or objects)

5. **Letter Writing** (Writing letters or one's own name on request)

6. **Phonological-Short-Term Memory** (Remembering spoken information for a short period of time)

You may be thinking...Those skills all seem so far away! My child isn't old enough to read yet. How can I facilitate his communication and future literacy skills at this age? Well, it's easy. Here are a few suggestions:

Introduce book reading as an enjoyable experience.
Choose books with simple pictures (either line drawings or real photos are ok). Text is not necessary, but familiarization with text is always beneficial. Choose a comfortable place where your child can easily see the book and still reference you. Be an enthusiastic reader. Use your voice and facial expressions to help your child notice the emotion of the character/picture and anticipate events (e.g., turning the page, something funny/silly happening to the character, etc.). Even an infant will enjoy looking at the pictures and responding to the changes in your voice and face as you talk about the doggie playing with the ball or daddy hugging the baby.

Read to your child frequently.
Establish a reading routine. Your child will enjoy reading to start or end the day, after a meal, before a nap, etc.

Help your child learn as you read.
Books provide a great opportunity to increase your child's vocabulary by introducing new words and concepts in a fun manner. Talk about the character's emotions and actions. Point out how events build upon one another to make a story (e.g., first, next, last). For infants this might be simply labeling objects, actions or feelings (e.g., ball, cup, Daddy's happy, Smile Daddy). As your child gets older, follow his lead. Talk about the pictures that he shows particular interest in. Ask him questions that help him connect his own life experience with the story or compares and contrasts the book with other books he has read. Ask your child about his favorite part of the book and share yours.

Choose books that help you teach.
Read many different kinds of books with characters and stories that are familiar as well as very different from your child's experiences. Use alphabet books to teach names of letters and sounds. Counting books are a fun and easy way to teach numbers and quantity concepts. (I personally love the books where you use cereal or other treats to demonstrate number concepts, then grab some energy with a snack.) Phonological (sound) awareness is easy to teach when you read poetry books or books that rhyme and books of different sizes (small books for infants and babies, larger books for toddlers and preschoolers) are great for teaching book handling skills.

Finally, *reread your child's favorite books.*
Children love to read books and tell the same stories over and over again. Rereading a book is a great way to maximize the potential in any communication. Think about it. When you reread the book, your child already knows the general storyline, characters, etc. This set knowledge will allow you to ask new and deeper questions about vocabulary, character attributes, story events, etc. Take advantage of the opportunity to find out more detail about why a particular book is your child's favorite. Ask him to continue the story. Encourage him to be creative! Even with your infant or baby, the benefits of prior knowledge will allow you to explore each picture in more detail and focus on language skills that are at your child's growing edge!

NOTES

Note 1:
Adapted from PRO-ED (1999) and Bleile (1995). See the "From Crying to Conversation" Worksheet at the end of the book for a more detailed list of communication developmental milestones. Parents keep in mind that the purpose of the above checklist is to provide general communication, speech and language milestones and a guide for typical acquisition ages; however, there is a generous range of acquisition for these skills that is still considered typical.

REFERENCES

Bleile, K. M. (1995). *Manual of articulation and phonological disorders.* San Diego, CA: Singular Publishing Group.

Brown, R. (1973). *A first language: The early stages.* Cambridge, MA: Harvard University Press.

Hegde, M. N. (1996). *Pocket guide to treatment in speech-language pathology.* San Diego, CA: Singular Publishing Group.

National Early Literacy Panel. (2008). *Developing early literacy: Report of the national early literacy panel.* Washington, DC: National Institute for Literacy.

Piaget, J. (1962). *Play, dreams and imitation in childhood.* New York: W. W. Norton & Co.

PRO-ED Inc. (1999). *Speech and language milestone chart.* TX: PRO-ED Inc.

Schwartz, R.G. and Leonard, L.B. (1982). *Do children pick and choose? An examination of phonological selection and avoidance in early lexical acquisition.* J of Child Language Jun; 9(2): 319-36.

10 Minutes for Talking

Made in the USA
Charleston, SC
18 November 2012